Every Second Counts

How to achieve business excellence, transform operational productivity and deliver extraordinary results

Top Right Thinking Ltd
www.toprightthinking.com
Cygnet Park, 4 Office Village, Forder Way,
Hampton, Peterborough, PE7 8GX

First published in Great Britain 2023.
Copyright © Simon Hedaux and Sue Hedaux

Designed and typeset by Noodle Juice Ltd.

ISBN: 978-1-916-0853-8-1

1 3 5 7 9 10 8 6 4 2

Every Second Counts

How to achieve business excellence, transform operational productivity and deliver extraordinary results

Sue Hedaux
Simon Hedaux

About the authors:

Simon Hedaux

Simon's retail career started in DIY as a part time job during college that turned into an opportunity to join the Boots Do It All management programme. After working in a range of stores and progressing to store manager, Simon developed his interest in getting resourcing right when he project managed the implementation and roll out of a workforce management system for the business that was by now called Focus DIY.

Simon dug further into resourcing when he went on to work for a leading workforce management system provider working across Europe to implement new scheduling systems with retailers.

In 2008 Simon joined Boots as Productivity Manager and took responsibility for the workload model that supported salary budgeting for all 2,500 Boots large stores and small pharmacies.

In 20111, Simon spotted a gap in the market – businesses that provided work measurement existed and strategic consultancies that helped improve productivity were well established – but what really creates lasting improvement is combining detailed analysis with a strategic business perspective to drive new value. And so, in 2011 Simon left Boots and ReThink Productivity was founded.

Simon is now a recognised expert supporting businesses across a range of sectors to address the core challenge of how organisations operate efficiently and optimise matching people resources to their workload. For three years Simon has produced the ReThink Productivity Podcast with a growing listener base and a mission to share practical ideas to improve productivity.

Sue Hedaux

After qualifying as a pharmacist, managing several stores, and supporting other managers operate their stores well as being an area manager at Boots, it was a natural step for Sue to specialise in productivity and efficiency at Head Office. Sue worked for a number of years at Boots in leadership roles across many parts over the business - commercial, finance and retail operations. Leading teams looking at product and fixturing development in beauty, workload modelling, workforce management system implementation and process efficiency, Sue faced many of the challenges that businesses are dealing with today. Productivity is a journey not a destination!

After a period working in the customer experience sector, while supporting ReThink as Co-Founder in her spare time, Sue joined ReThink full-time in 2019. She now combines her twin passions for efficiency and customer experience by surfacing insights that help businesses make better informed decisions.

Sue leads the team who deliver onsite data capture, analysis, insights, and workload models for ReThink.

Whether you are a seasoned executive or just starting the journey in management this book has something for everyone . As someone who has been managing people for 50 plus years, the book reminded me of some fundamentals and indeed made me consider my current processes. Well done on writing a book that is simple, supported by great examples and case studies and will have several nuggets that will improve every business, big or small.

Nigel Travis
Principal Challenge Consulting LLC

What a great accessible read, so many ideas and pointers contained in an easily digestible book, Every Second Counts really is a handbook for productivity success for anyone starting out on this business-critical journey. Full of helpful hints, suggestions and ways to get started on driving efficiency in your business, allowing the team to enjoy their work more, serve their customers better and deliver long term financial success for the business.

Jason Cotta
CEO, Lagkagehuset | Ole & Steen

This book is invaluable reading for anyone in retail. For a self-confessed non-expert in WFM, but an analyst and commentator on bricks and mortar retailing, I found it fascinating and extremely helpful in unravelling and simplifying the complexities of optimising retail ops processes. Also the structure of the book is easy to understand and navigate, enabling readers to dip into different chapters which are relevant to their immediate needs. An essential bit of a retailer's toolkit!

Diane Wehrle SFIPM

Marketing and Insights Director at MRI Springboard

In short, sharp, practical chapters, this book distils the essence of productivity in the workplace. Essential reading for those starting out and key reminders for those of us who have been there and done that!

Dulcie Swanston FCIPD

Managing Director Tea Break Training,
Executive Coach and Author

For our ReThink team and clients – past, present and future...

Contents

Introduction

Are you the sort of person who enjoys finding better ways to do things? Does your job require you to find more productive ways of getting things done? Or do you have to find ways to create capacity to explore new business ideas? If so, this book will help you answer the key questions you will be asking yourself.

There are many books written on time management and personal productivity, providing useful skills and techniques to help individuals be more effective – this book is different. It is aimed at people who help organisations perform more effectively. You probably have productivity, processes or continuous improvement in your job spec and perhaps even in your job title. You are likely in an operations or transformation team tasked with finding ways of releasing time from the operation to meet the ongoing productivity challenge every organisation faces. This practical handbook will help you identify and quantify the stream of productivity improvements required year after year.

Built around questions frequently asked by our clients, this book gives you the information you need to address your day-to-day challenges. You will find interesting case studies and quick-win steps, getting you off to a flying start.

If you are new to a role that requires you finding and implementing productivity improvements, you might want to read each chapter carefully from beginning to end. However, for most, you will be able to dip into a chapter that deals with your specific challenge. Each chapter is free standing and does not rely on information presented previously.

When considering the case studies and quick wins, remember productivity needs to work in the context of your business. What is your business strategy? What are your brand values? What are the short and long-term targets for the organisation? Productivity improvement is about doing things better for your unique brand. Anything else can be brand-damaging cost-cutting. It can be a fine balance between operational innovation and making changes that devalue the brand for your clients.

At **ReThink**, we set out to help businesses create better decisions for positive change. We hope this book supports you to make evidence-based decisions that drive your organisation forward.

Chapter 1

Where is your money really going?

(Or how are you *really* spending your money?)

For most businesses, people are one of the biggest investments an organisation makes. The salary budget line can be tens of millions of pounds for a large retail chain and much smaller for a start-up fast-food chain; whatever the size of your business, salaries are likely to be a large portion of your cost base.

It's not just because it's a lot of money that means your people budget is important. The investment you make in salaries determines the experience felt by your end customers and how well you land your business strategy. How often does salary budgeting feel like a chore? If you reframe it as a one-off opportunity to invest in differentiating your brand from your competitors, it feels a much more urgent and important task to turn your attention to.

Getting budgeting right also impacts employee experience. A whole range of important things come together to create employee experience. People may often overlook how accurately the hours allocated through the budgeting process match actual demand. It is gruelling to work in a business where there are just not enough hours to cover the workload, making every day a tough mountain to climb. Equally soul destroying is working in a business where there is just not enough to do, leaving colleagues with hours of endless boredom and a lack of motivation to achieve anything. The 'just right' pressure of work creates an environment that feels dynamic and energising while still having enough time to support new people easing into their roles and experienced team members to grow into their next one.

Once you have made considered budget allocations by site, and by week, that reflect your opportunities for revenue growth and the way you want your customers and employees to experience your business, how do you know what happens to those carefully allocated hours when they are spent? Does that investment go where you want it to?

Salary budgeting is an act of caring for your customers and your teams, so it deserves to shake off the dull spreadsheet image.

Some businesses have tools that can help them shape how time is invested on a day to day and hour by hour basis – they can be everything from Excel based shift and rota plans through to very complex software that allocates resource by fifteen-minute intervals. Finding and implementing the right solution for your business is even harder than saying the mouthful that is the generic name for these tools – workforce management software, or WFM for short. Even with all that planning, the end result of how well your people budget is invested is only as good as the decisions made by your site managers.

Consequently, most businesses may not really know where their salary budget is invested. Is the allocated money for a new customer advisor role that will differentiate the service you provide and drive sales going where you think it is? Or has a store manager decided they need more hours to get stock on the shelf and swallowed up the extra hours into behind-the-scenes tasks? Have local managers with the best of intentions not managed to execute the investment to best effect? For example, if you allocate extra money to cover a Click and Collect or delivery service with a one-hour guarantee, do managers make it happen? It might be they get a huge peak demand for orders to be picked at a certain time of day that is difficult to recruit for. Or unpredictable deliveries might pull colleagues away from other customer facing tasks you'd rather they were doing.

Running an operation is like trying to constantly ride a fast-moving wave – requiring an eye on the horizon with constant micro adjustments to keep riding the wave and avoiding an embarrassing tumble into the surf.

If understanding how to plan and implement your money and time spending to benefit your customers is difficult, how can you know how your money is spent?

How do I find out?

The only way to really know how salary budgets are spent is to measure it onsite. One tried and tested approach is by using old-fashioned-sounding time and motion studies, where specially trained analysts record what they see in the business. A diagnostic measurement of how your team spends time over the course of the day and week will show you how your budget spend is split across the tasks the team completes and how your budgeted colleague hours are deployed versus the customer demand. Here are some of key questions you could answer.

- How much time are you spending with your customers versus completing head down tasks?

- Are the hours allocated for a strategic investment actually in place?

- How long do you spend moving and counting stock?

- How much admin do your teams do?

- What extra work do area managers give your teams to do?

- Where are your teams and managers across the day? On the sales floor assisting and selling to customers or static behind a counter? Or are they sitting in an office?

- How much downtime is there when the team numbers on shift outstrip the work they have to do?

At a top line, the output will tell you what proportion of time, as a percentage, is spent on the tasks that add value for your business.

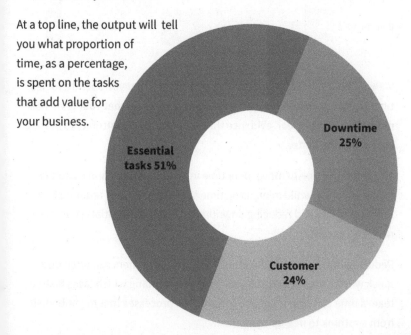

Essential tasks 51%

Downtime 25%

Customer 24%

If the chart on the previous page was for your business, you now know your team spends only a quarter of their time with customers; are you pleased or disappointed with that?

This is where benchmarking can help. It gives you a context for your own business metrics and creates a useful 'outside in' perspective. The chart below represents a generic business that sells products and services to customers.

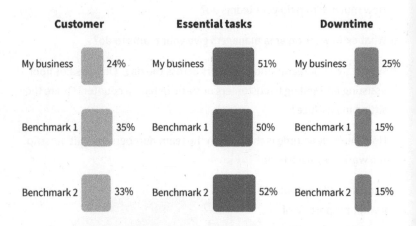

Customer		Essential tasks		Downtime	
My business	24%	My business	51%	My business	25%
Benchmark 1	35%	Benchmark 1	50%	Benchmark 1	15%
Benchmark 2	33%	Benchmark 2	52%	Benchmark 2	15%

Viewing this chart for your business, you will see that you spend a lot less time with your customers than your competitors and that your team has more downtime – clear evidence that you have an opportunity to make a change for the better.

The aim should be to move more time into value-adding and customer-facing activities while minimising time spent on the tasks required for the business to run and reducing downtime to just the essentials your team needs for breaks.

Reducing downtime and directing it towards customers can often be a quick win for improving productivity. Understanding which tasks take your team's time can help point you towards the processes that might benefit from a rethink to free up more time.

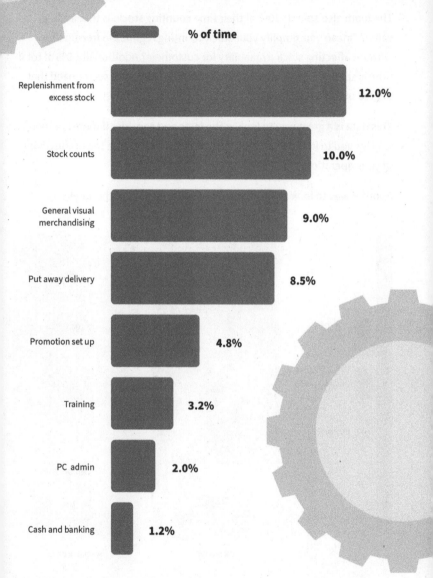

% of time

Category	%
Replenishment from excess stock	12.0%
Stock counts	10.0%
General visual merchandising	9.0%
Put away delivery	8.5%
Promotion set up	4.8%
Training	3.2%
PC admin	2.0%
Cash and banking	1.2%

This chart shows that less time is spent putting the delivery away than filling up from excess stock later – which probably means stock levels are too high in store and moving to a more "just in time" approach for stock could free up a colleague's time.

The team also spends 10% of their time counting stock. Is that adding value? Or can you simplify your stock counting regimes to free up time without affecting stock availability for customers? Additionally, 9% of total time is spent on displays and merchandising. Does your sector need that degree of display change?

This data is a great way to look at the facts and consider if there is a better way for you to invest your people resources and increase the productivity of your operation.

Another way to look at your data is to view it by days of the week.

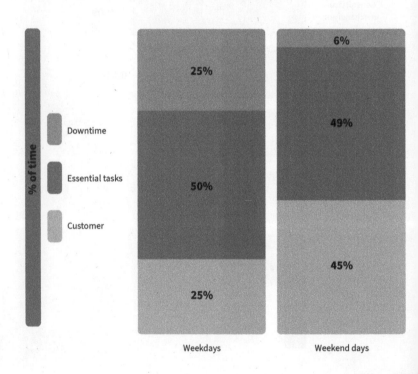

This simple view shows that weekdays have lower customer time and higher levels of downtime, showing that there are more colleagues on shift than needed on weekdays. The exact opposite is true for busier weekend days where the higher customer time and low downtime suggests an opportunity to move resources to the weekend to grow sales. This data really helps with the practical decisions business leaders have to make every day – where do I invest my resources?

You can get some top-line data by carrying out these sorts of observations yourself, however, do you really have the time to send some of your own team out to record observations? Bringing in trained analysts who make the observations and analyse the data for you creates the opportunity for a fresh pair of expert eyes on the operation. Observational feedback on best practice and opportunities to improve efficiency from productivity experts as they capture data onsite adds an extra dimension. Then combine their feedback with data to create a list of quantified efficiency opportunities specific to your unique business.

Simple measurement gives you powerful insights that help you direct improvement projects to where they will make the most difference, creating a feedback loop that shows whether hours are invested in the way you intended.

What different investment choices would you make if you knew these numbers for your business?

Case Studies – How others have used this data.

Output diagnostic measurement is often the stimulus for a wider review of how a business operates.

Example 1:

A business providing an expert B2B service found that only 10% of total time was spent on the part of the service that their clients valued.

Their established ways of working meant that a highly paid expert would manage their projects end to end – yet this meant that only 10% of their time added value and the rest of the time was doing the necessary admin work that was required to set up the service.

As is often the case, a diagnostic study confirmed the view of the senior manager that change was needed. The data changed the issue from a senior manager's theory to an evidence-based fact that allowed discussions to design a change programme. The business is now looking at how admin support can be added in to free up experts in the short-term and how systems and ways of working can be updated to automate as many of the data flows and required admin work as possible.

With these baseline measures now established, it will be easy for the company to use diagnostic tests to measure the progress they make and identify the next opportunity hotspots to target.

Example 2:

A grocery retailer saw that they spent twice as long filling up from the excess stock they held off the sales floor compared to time spent processing their delivery and putting stock directly onto the shelves. This simple statistic pointed to the fact that they could rethink their stock operation and release significant time in store to invest in activities customers value much more than a colleague moving the same item of stock multiple times.

This insight prompted a review of the stock operation across the business. Ideal stock processes are designed so stock is touched as few times as possible – preferably just once in store to put it on the shelf before the customer buys it. Every extra touch takes additional time, increases the cost to sell and reduces net profit. The company worked to reduce stock cover over time so they could work with the warehouse to manage their space, protect shelf availability for customers in the store, and release time from stock handling.

Supply challenges have remained a reality since COVID-19 interrupted global supply chains and many businesses have increased stock cover as a result. An initially sensible precaution during a pandemic has become, in some instances, an embedded way of working. Understanding the workload and cost trade-offs if high volumes of stock are pushed through to stores allows a business to make better and more nuanced decisions.

Example 3:

A kitchen retailer in Europe deployed one role within their showrooms to cover everything, from monitoring the sales pipeline and chasing up leads, creating designs, through to being available for browsing customers and keeping the showroom clean and shiny. You can probably guess that a diagnostic measurement combined with observation proved that the way the job role was designed did not set the job holders up for success, spreading them too thinly across all the tasks that play a part in driving sales.

Analysis and observation showed:

- The concentration required for designing kitchens and creating quotes meant that they did not have the awareness of potential customers browsing the showroom. Most customers browsing the show room area were therefore unacknowledged and potential sales leads slipped away.

- Insufficient attention was paid to the showroom displays so they did not look their best in creating the image of a dream kitchen.

- Benchmarking of this operation versus similar ones showed that while this business had one role trying to do everything, other similar businesses had two roles. One role as a specialist kitchen designer able to dedicate time for home visits and hour-long in-store design sessions to close the deal. With a second role as an assistant who is available to speak with browsing customers, ensure the showroom always looks its best and provides admin support too.

You might be thinking that this is so blindingly obvious, why didn't the business already realise it? The reality is that senior leaders are often busy with multiple priorities fighting for their time and attention and after a while, it becomes hard to envision an operation running different to the way it already does.

The best insights to surface are the ones that, with the benefit of measurement, stand out clearly because they have the power to transform an operation and drive a significant difference for the business.

Quick wins – what you can do now.

Bringing in productivity experts to your business allows a fresh look at your operation, but you might not be able to do that. You can access some quick wins yourself, though, if you can adopt that 'outside-in' view too. A great way to start is to visit competitor businesses if you can. It helps to broaden your view and see different ways of doing things. If you can free your mind from tasks requiring your immediate attention and take some time to stand back and watch your operation, you will observe some of the signs and symptoms that point to opportunities.

- Queues are a sign of unmet demand and point to an opportunity to grow sales if you can increase your capacity at peak times.

- Do you have most of your experienced team members working on the busiest days and times? Sundays remain the most intense trading hours for retail in the UK due to the constraints on opening times, and still present growth opportunities for many businesses.

- Ask your teams and your team leaders what they think takes them away from adding value for the business and you will quickly gather a list of great ideas to implement with new challenges to tackle.

- How do you launch new initiatives in your business? Do projects or concepts get launched while leaving teams to work out how to fit them in alongside all their other jobs? Or is there good consideration of any extra work that might be required?

Chapter 2

How can I serve more customers at peak times?

Peak trading is the most important time for you, your teams and your customers; getting it right can make or break your business.

Commercially, it is critical that you get your peak trading periods right as that is when you make the most profit. Historically, for a lot of retailers, the profit for a whole year of trading rests on the few weeks running up to Christmas. Retailers who sell gift orientated products like fragrance and children's toys can make over half their sales for the year between October and December. Garden centres, DIY stores and pubs with great outdoor eating spaces boom from Easter through to autumn – if the weather is kind to them. Fitness related businesses get a boost as we all make our new year resolutions, then see customer numbers decline as will power fades. When peaks happen varies by industry and they are always business critical.

There are demand peaks that create an annual rhythm for many businesses; there are also peaks within a week and even a day. For example, most retail and leisure operations find the weekend daytime to be busier than a wet Wednesday. Businesses supplying coffee and lunches for busy commuters can experience up to three huge peaks a day – the essential morning coffee on the way to work, a lunchtime sandwich and a hot drink for the journey home.

Your peak times are when there are the most customers looking for the sort of service you provide.

So, if you are looking to grab new customers and grow your sales, it's the perfect time to be at your best, delivering great products and service. A sandwich shop is going to find it a lot easier to pick up a few extra customers around lunchtime with an enticing display and a fast-moving customer line. Understanding when customers are in the market for what you have to offer is the easiest way to grow your business, but making sure you are operationally ready for the peak takes planning and requires good execution of the plan.

It is obviously true that your busiest times are when the highest number of customers experience what it is like to do business with you. That makes it the most important time to get everything right with your operation. This is not the time for long, slow queues and empty shelves. You need the right number of colleagues on shift to serve customers and minimise queues. Products need to be on the shelves and as many routine tasks cleared out of the way to be completed at a quieter time, meaning your team can focus on your customers during that important peak time.

You'll have shared the frustration of standing in a queue while the store team prioritised moving stock around instead of looking after you. Or even worse, had colleagues move you out of the way while you were trying to grab your shopping because someone had given them a deadline to get the delivery on the shelf and experienced service desks closing for colleague breaks just as the queue is starting to build. Good operators prioritise looking after customers at peak times and arrange everything else around important busy periods – including all chores and breaks. Getting all that right means teams are ready to go as the peak starts then can jump into recovery mode as soon as the peak tails off.

Unless you've tried to do it, it sounds easy to set yourself up for peak. If you have run a business through a busy time, you will know there are lots of things conspiring to make it a constantly moving target rather than something you achieve once, then just press repeat. A million and one things can make it hard to be at your best for every peak – just ask the coffee shop manager whose milk delivery doesn't turn up, or the retailers who had time sensitive products held up when a container ship became wedged across the Suez Canal, bringing chaos to international shipping lines in 2021. A huge challenge is that it isn't easy to recruit people to work the part time hours that help you ramp up your colleague numbers for the busy times, so you have to work out how to plan all your tasks so that you have shift patterns that are workable for your team as well as your customers. It's like trying to build the perfect picture with jigsaw pieces that keep shape shifting and spontaneously moving around.

It is the perpetual operational challenge.

Pulling together output diagnostics, ensuring good team numbers and refining your team to be effective so that products are available on shelves before peak, breaks are dealt with before or after peak, will delight your customers and keep them coming back. Being able to run a tight ship requires observation and good planning so you can deal with the disruptions that will inevitably come your way. Operations leaders are well advised to heed the 18th century sentiment often ascribed to Benjamin Franklin, "If you fail to prepare, you are preparing to fail."

Despite everything, you keep tweaking your operation and growing your customer numbers until one day you reach the point where you have maxed out your capacity and can't take any more customers at peak without either providing a poorer experience or overwhelming your team. What then? How do you take the pressure off and create more capacity for growth?

How can I serve more customers at peak times?

It's time to take a hard look at how long it takes to do things in your business. How long it takes to do things at peak matters because if you can reduce the time required to look after each customer, you could serve many more customers with the same resources.

Look at the activities that your team have to repeat over and over again as these are the ones with the most time saving potential. It could be serving a customer at a till, making hot food and drinks in a busy quick-serve restaurant or picking orders for delivery from a warehouse. Taking a few seconds off something you do a thousand times a day creates extra capacity just when you need it most.

To spot the second-saving opportunities, you need to take a close look at your processes. It helps to know exactly how long each step of the process takes and to be able to identify any bottle necks that cause delays. You can do some of this yourself by observing your operation when it is running at peak. And time and motion study experts will get you to the next level of detail with careful measurement of the tasks your team are doing.

Most things we do can be broken down into series of smaller steps that add up to the overall service you provide for your customer. Understanding these process steps and how long each one takes helps you know where to direct your efforts. The stage that takes the longest is the one to look at first because speeding it up will have the biggest impact on your overall time to serve a customer or complete the task.

Let's look at the coffee making process below. Once you know that frothing milk and mixing the shot with water, milk and syrups takes the most time, you should focus your time saving efforts there. The other good thing about knowing these times for each step is it encourages you to look at more radical solutions such as considering removing a step completely. What if more customers placed their own order and paid via your app? Or via a kiosk instore as lots of fast-food outlets do? Or could you automate any of the drink-making processes?

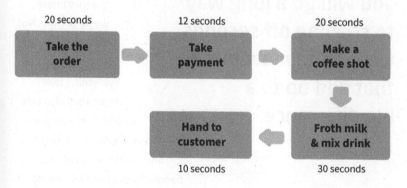

In addition to giving you process times, time and motion studies can also measure the impact of disruptions that cause delays for customers. For example, how often does a team member have to break off from their task to answer the telephone, or walk away to get something they need? Have you ever bought a phone in a store and waited while the colleague walks to a distant printer to get essential paperwork and then had another wait while they run to a downstairs stock room to get your phone? When things work smoothly, observing the flow of activity is like watching a choreographed troupe in action and everything just seems to work. Delays and disruptions caused by unnecessary movement can be easy to spot if you stand back. Movements that look jarring to an observer are probably due to extra movements because the work doesn't flow as well as it could.

Things out of place mean that colleagues have to walk further, reach awkwardly, or even worse have to go and hunt down an essential bit of kit that someone else has walked away with. Searching for a pen or scissors that aren't there when you need them is a frustrating waste of time. Not only do these extra movements make everything take longer, they also take their toll on your team. Every extra twist, bend and stretch means people become more tired and creates a risk of repetitive strain injury.

If you apply the adage 'a place for everything and everything in its place' to your work areas, you will go a long way to shaving off seconds from extra movements that add up to a big difference.

Examples of things out of place include printers situated a walk away producing a label or document you need. Cupboards that open outwards so the colleague must step back rather than a sliding door they can open without moving, and shelves set just too high, meaning some colleagues have to fetch a step ladder or attempt a risky stretch to get the item they need. It is quicker to be able to work one handed rather than needing two – because a one-handed movement requires less effort and co-ordination and allows the other hand to move onto the next task more efficiently. We all know how much quicker it is to get a piece of Sellotape from a dispenser with a single, one-handed movement rather trying to find the end of the Sellotape with one hand as you hold it with the other. Once you start looking for things slightly out of place in your operation you will find lots of examples.

Time spent moving to reach what you need has the most dramatic effect on time to complete a task in warehouses and stock moving operations. In a warehouse where items are selected from the shelves to assemble an order, traveling up and down aisles between storage locations can be up to half of the total time for the job. Simple solutions like making sure the most frequently picked items are easiest to reach and close to the despatch area are a good start. The use of clever technology helps with trickier things such as making sure the order that items are shown on the picking list match the layout of the warehouse can make a big difference to how long it takes to pick an individual order. Speeding up time taken for a single order in turn drives the maximum number of orders a warehouse can despatch in a day and increases capacity at peak, making a huge difference when the rush is on.

You'll spot lots of time saving opportunities with a careful look at your own operation. Adding in an external perspective with benchmarking opens up even more possibilities. If benchmarking shows that your peers can complete a process in half the time you can, it pushes you to be more radical than if you are comfortably sitting in middle of the pack.

If you tackle just one productivity challenge, getting things as efficient as you can during peak is the place to start.

Case Studies - How others have used this data.

A series of small changes can create a big difference overall.

When Sir Dave Brailsford was Performance Director at British Cycling, he believed that if you make a 1% improvement in a host of tiny areas, the cumulative benefits would be extraordinary. After years of cycling mediocrity, British Cycling became a global force to be reckoned with, all down to the strategy of "the aggregation of marginal gains". [1]

That same strategy has worked wonders for many organisations who have taken the time to really look at what they do.

Example 1:

A coffee shop specialising in serving coffees to commuters rushing through a station wanted to improve their productivity. The aggregation of marginal gains here added up to increased capacity so they could make 25% more hot drinks in any given hour. That's a huge operational change that translated into increased sales. How was it done? Simple changes meant setting up a workstation with everything to hand, such

---

1 Brailsford, D., cited in Syed, M., (2015) *Black Box Thinking* [publisher information].

as: angling paper cups so they are easier to grab from a stack, setting up syrups so they can be dispensed one handed, and switching away from plastic milk bottles like those we all struggle to get the seal off. A bigger change was introducing automation, with a machine that automatically ground coffee beans and created the coffee shot, allowing the colleagues to focus on frothing milk and making the drinks. Most customers dashing through a station are prepared to trade off a hand-ground hot coffee for a consistently good one that gets them on their way faster.

Example 2:

A warehouse team getting bulk stock from racking onto pallets that would go out as deliveries were travelling long distances up and down aisles in the warehouse. A series of small changes that offered opportunities to speed things up included:

- creating a one-way system that kept everyone moving the same direction and prevented colleagues getting in each other's way

- moving frequently picked items so they were on a core route through the racks

- storing boxes and pallets so they used the depth of the racking for efficient storage and reduced the overall distance travelled.

This aggregation of marginal gains added up to a 15% productivity improvement. A huge shift in a business sector that constantly deals with low operating margins and ever-increasing costs.

Example 3:

A grocery retailer with a significant lunch offer experienced big queues during the lunchtime peak. It wasn't just demand for lunch items from the counter that went up, it was across the store as people who dashed out of work during their lunch break were shopping for other things they needed too. Self-checkout tills were an obvious way to increase the capacity to serve customers. Getting the introduction of self-checkout tills right is not easy. How many to put in, where to put them and how to efficiently provide help for customers when they need it without having a colleague hanging around just in case they are needed is an art as well as a science. The good news is that when customers take on average three to four minutes to self-serve at a self-checkout, each unit added creates capacity to serve an extra fifteen to twenty customers an hour at peak times. If managed well and balanced correctly with the total service capacity, it can make a big difference to customer queue lengths and create capacity to grow sales.

Quick Wins – What you can do now.

Watch your operation at peak to see what gets in the way of your team helping as many customers as possible.

- What extra movements do the team make? Get the layout right and standardise how everyone works to eliminate non-essential activity.

- What interrupts the smooth flow of the process? Anything that creates stops and starts slows down your process; moving things around to prevent interruptions will increase capacity.

- Process steps that require a supervisor's authorisation are worth a look too – train your team so they don't need to be checked on and authorised, saving yours and your customer's time, removing the need to wait for someone else to double check what they are doing.

- Identify slow points causing extra customer delays or stopping team members in other parts of the process as they wait for the slowest step to catch up to them.

- Are the team trying to get other jobs completed during busy times? Move anything that can wait to a different time of your peak period. Whether that is your daily peak, or the peak in your annual business cycle.

Look for bottle necks.

- Have you given your team the training they need to be as efficient as they can? Would a bit of extra support and coaching help colleagues be more productive?

- Who is running the operation at peak? A leader who helps clear obstacles as they arise ensures smooth running.

Chapter 3

How can I make savings?

Making savings has a bad reputation. In many peoples' minds it is associated with a slash and burn approach that saves money but damages customer experience and even the long-term viability of the operation. It can sound like desperate measures, and sometimes is.

That's not the sort of savings we endorse. We need to move on to a more nuanced and frankly, grown-up debate about making savings.

Financial advisors advocate we should all know where our own money is going and review our regular outgoings so we can keep a good grip on our personal finances. We should make sure we don't have the monthly insurance cost for a mobile phone that we swapped out ages ago and shop around for the best deal for utilities, insurances and more. Managing costs in things we have to pay for, like a mortgage deal, hopefully means we have a little more to spend on the fun stuff like holidays. Or that we are saving for something big we want to do – like put an extension on the house, or save for our children's first car, university fees or wedding. A whole sector has developed to make sure we can easily compare costs on the services we buy. Most banks now offer their customers the ability to tag and track spending by different categories as part of the basic toolkit for managing our own finances. Many banks also offer the opportunity to set up separate saving pots, so we can have dedicated spaces for saving for our next holiday, new car, or upcoming bills. It's all designed to help us know where our money is going and to be able to allocate funds to the things that are important to us.

Looking for savings in a business context is applying those same principles of good money management on a larger scale. It's just as important to get it right for a business. If you get your budgeting wrong at home, maybe you'll have to wait another year for the new kitchen or give the movie package on Sky a miss. Get it wrong in a business operating on tight margins, in a competitive market with a tricky economic environment to contend with and the whole business could falter – along with employee jobs and the service they provide to customers who have come to rely on them.

> **Saving is not a dirty word, it's just common sense and a duty within any responsible company.**

The sort of saving that is related to the ongoing tweaking of spend to make sure investment goes where it has the biggest positive impact is good management – it's like checking you have got a good price for the insurance coverage you need at home.

Sometimes you need to free up spending from the core operation to support the business to have the cash to make new investment elsewhere. That might be developing a new product or service or opening new locations. This is the saving that's like trimming your weekly outgoings to put money aside for a bigger spend on a holiday.

And sometimes you just need to urgently make a saving. Something unexpected has happened with your cash flow and to get through the next few months you have to reduce outgoings. There can be lots of reasons triggering this sort of saving requirement in business.

It's the equivalent of your washing machine breaking down or an unexpected big bill for your car.

So, let's all accept that looking for savings is something that should be fundamental in our work routines and is part of what well run businesses do to be able to invest in new ideas that fuel their growth and long-term success. Ideally a business will have what we call a productivity roadmap. That's a multiyear plan that shows any known additional costs that are going to come along combined with a series of initiatives that create savings that balance out the planned expenditure increases. These plans usually have more planned projects and detail in the short term and are a little sketchy if looked at too far ahead. The discipline of keeping a productivity roadmap means you know what savings you need to find and the value of process improvements you need deliver in plenty of time. Take the example on the next page...

Initiative	This year	Next year	The year after
Big IT project	Define requirements, select vendor and trial	Roll out phase 1 Benefit delivery: **£££**	Roll out phase 2 Benefit delivery: **££**
Consumables	Quick win – supplier tender process to reduce cost. Save 10% of budget. Develop options to avoid use of consumables.	Test and roll out. Benefit delivery: 75% of budget.	
Stock handling costs	Quick win – flag promotional stock inbound to reduce sortation at store. Benefit delivery: **£**	Update store tech to speed up stock processes. Benefit delivery: **££** Work with Distribution Centre on joint project to reduce stock handling across the organisation. Implement quick wins: **£**	Roll out DC and store stock process changes. Benefit delivery: **£££££**
Quick wins	Stop stock counts Benefit delivery: **£** Introduce app to minimise waste: **££**	Identify next set of quick wins	

The worst way to deliver savings is to make a blunt percentage cost reduction across any spend you can, which usually includes salary spend. To a degree, companies got away with this in the past because we didn't use to run our businesses as close to the bone, as we tend to now. There might have been some slack in the system that a blanket cut tightened up, and everything could still run as normal. Most businesses will tell you, those days are long gone.

The only way to achieve salary cost savings while avoiding a negative impact on customers and the business integrity is to remove work. Taking out an unnecessary process is essential for taking out cost.

So where do you start?

Making the savings

The first place to start looking to reduce salary spend, is to know how time – and therefore money – is spent in your operation. You probably set budgets with the best of intentions of how the cash should be spent. Head office plans aren't always implemented the way you might hope by the time the message has gone through layers of management and then ends up with a local manager with a strong conviction about the best way to run their part of the business. Good intentions and even a great plan don't always mean that time is used how you planned it to be. So, knowing what is really happening gives you a good place to start.

Trained work study analysts can use what used to be known as time and motion studies to measure how time is actually spent. Work study brings experts in to measure your operational processes and how time is spent so you can pinpoint downtime and benchmark how you do things versus your peers.

In work study we split activity in to three broad categories.

1. Customer-facing, value-adding time

Usually you want to maximise the amount of time spent in customer-facing tasks, as this drives better customer experiences and revenue.

2. Essential tasks and processes

This is time spent doing the things that have to be done for the operation to function. It can be putting stock on the shelves in a shop or warehouse, the cleaning that must be done in a food outlet or processing paperwork and completing admin tasks. The challenge here is to find ways to get these essential jobs done as quickly and cost effectively as possible by your own team or an outsourced partner. Freeing up time from tasks is like saving money on your mobile phone bill – you get everything you need and free up some cash to put into a savings pot.

3. Downtime

This is often the source of quick win savings. Downtime happens when more resources have been allocated than are required to meet the demand and workload. It is the time when there are more colleagues on shift than customers in the shop or cafe. Or it can be when the team are all there ready to put the delivery away and the driver is running late again and won't be there for another hour. Downtime can be waiting for customers when there is nothing else to do, chatting about anything other than work to fill the dead time, or it can be doing a job that doesn't really need doing but is better than doing nothing. Have you been in a beauty hall when it is quiet and seen how much dusting of already immaculate displays is happening?

Bringing in work study experts to spend time in a sample of your stores to measure how time is spent is a great way to understand what actually happens and identify where to focus your cost saving efforts. A diagnostic measure looking at how time is spent by the full team across the operating hours of the business gives you the info you need to know to start to make effective decisions.

The business in this chart spends a third of their time with customers and almost a quarter of time on downtime. That means that up to 25p in every pound that is invested in salary is lost as downtime because there are more colleagues on shift than customer numbers and the available work to do require. This is an easy place to find savings as too much resource is deployed for the level of customer time and tasks that need completing.

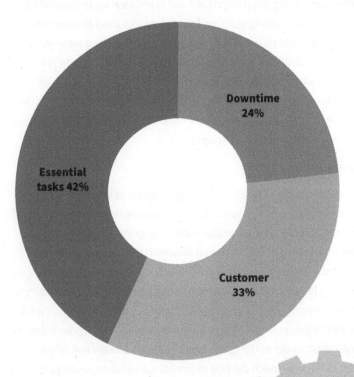

Downtime 24%

Essential tasks 42%

Customer 33%

Diagnostic studies work best when they cover a mix of outlets that reflect any differences that exist across your business. For example, different store formats and location types might not have the same issues. And businesses that have grown through acquisition usually have carry over ways of working from the old ownership that create different efficiency opportunities.

In the chart below, edge of town retail park stores have much higher downtime than the high street and regional shopping centre stores. This shows there is an opportunity to reduce salary spend in edge of town stores and reduce non-productive downtime.

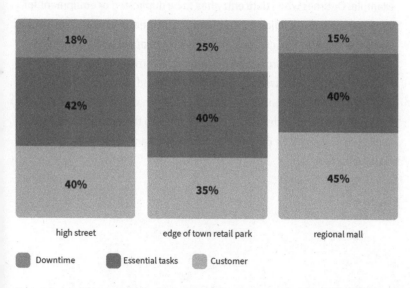

| high street | edge of town retail park | regional mall |

■ Downtime   ■ Essential tasks   ■ Customer

Downtime is the enemy of productivity. It is colleague time and business money spent without any productive output. Minimising downtime and maximising time on things customers value drives productivity

Data can be split by day of week, time of day, store size, store sales turnover or any other factor that influences productivity. The aim is to surface insights that help you make the best savings decisions for your business.

This diagnostic analysis becomes even more powerful when benchmarked against comparable businesses as it helps you to know how you stack up in your sector. Whether you are the top performer in the group and need to innovate to stay ahead or are at the bottom with some catching up to do, benchmarking is often a powerful board room motivator to invest effort to improve productivity.

Work study experts notice all sorts of things that can help your business be more efficient and the observations they provide from site also go into the mix when looking for the best opportunities to focus on. They might spot layout challenges that mean workers have to walk too far to a printer for example. Or times when data entry has to be duplicated or equipment for stock handling is not efficient. Combining data measurement, observations and benchmarking can create a quantified list of opportunities that will form the bedrock of a productivity roadmap. By sizing the opportunities and combining it with assessment of the effort and cost needed to make the change, you can identify quick wins to make happen faster and longer-term projects that will deliver savings for you into the future. It all comes back to optimising time on value-adding activity and minimising time on essential tasks.

Once you know how much time goes into your biggest chunks of work, you can start to focus where you can make the biggest difference.

Case Studies – How others have reduced costs.

Establishing a baseline though work study measurement has given businesses both a plan to make changes and a point to refer back to when assessing how effective change has been.

Example 1:

A budget retailer had experienced rapid growth and focused their operational efforts on opening new stores, as sales grew and grew. When sales are fuelled by new openings, the sales growth eventually starts to flatten out as it becomes harder to find suitable new sites. The bigger the network becomes, the tougher it is to find genuine new growth that doesn't pull sales from existing stores and good sites to develop.

As the chain grew in size but revenue growth started to slow down, the retailer realised that the systems and ways of working that had served them well as a small but fast-growing sales force were creaking in an estate many times larger than when they started out. Work study showed there was significant variation in how stores operated, and they knew it was time to get more scientific about how they did things. The business had a good model for how many colleagues were needed to open a new site, and less of a handle on how many hours are needed to operate each store cost-effectively as they reached maturity.

Diagnostic measurement showed how millions of pounds of opportunities could be unlocked through adopting one best way of operating their stores, combined with workload-based allocation of salary budgets.

This understanding didn't just help their existing stores. It also meant that new stores could operate with a lower cost base than before, so potential store sites that had looked to be marginally profitable to date became better options for new store openings.

Example 2:

Pharmacy chains are working hard to manage costs while facing into a unique set of challenges. A regulated environment, the need to deploy qualified professionals and fees set by the government limit their ability to make productivity changes that might be considered by other businesses.

Pharmacies have already exploited the quick wins open to them so were looking at new ways to operate. Quantifying time spent on essential tasks creates a framework for them to explore more innovative solutions for completing the work they need to do. Automation and robotics are increasingly being deployed by pharmacy chains, so the local teams are freed up to provide extra services for their local communities. By measuring process times and calculating cost, pharmacy chains can make the sums add up so they can invest in the technology that means pharmacy teams have the capacity to support the health of the nation.

Example 3:

A multi-national retailer recognised there were disparities in their operation between the different countries they operated in. They wanted to learn from the best practice already out there in some locations and benchmark their operation against other similar businesses.

Work study showed that some operational variance was driven by genuine differences in how customers shopped across continents. It also highlighted the differences where adopting one best way of operating would improve productivity. Additionally, sharing the outputs with the market leadership gave them the evidence base for them to adopt a more clear-eyed look at their own operation. The insights and observations helped each market generate ideas and take ownership for how they could improve their productivity. The work study project established a good framework for how country leaders could work with the global brand team and their peers to deliver more for the brand in their own market.

Quick Wins – What you can do now.

They are often changes that can also do wonders for your environmental footprint too.

Your business has probably had a cost saving or productivity programme running for years. While it can seem daunting to find fresh savings year after year, the fast-paced changes to the environment that we live and operate in means there are always new cost saving opportunities to exploit. Quick wins can provide an opportunity to make immediate savings.

Potential quick wins that reduce costs and are also good for the long term include:

- Consider the operational cost lines that aren't salary related, such as goods not for resale – that is costs for items used in the operation such as bags and cleaning materials, and uniforms. Many businesses can reduce paper costs by reducing the length of receipts or moving to make them on request and reducing printing. There can be significant costs savings in this area with better buying and rationalising what you use.

- Energy costs look set to remain a hot topic into the future fuelled by high electricity costs and wider environmental concerns. Many businesses use high levels of refrigeration and / or heating in addition to costs associated with moving stock around the country. Effective use of all the resources used by businesses as well as salary spend is important to consider. Simple things like putting in movement activated lighting in less-used areas can reduce costs while providing illumination when it is needed.

- High stock holding ties up cashflow, often incurs additional costs to store and every extra touch adds to the handling costs. Can you reduce stock holding on some lines to free up cash and reduce stock handling rework?

- Opening hours for customer facing operations drive salary and other costs. The balance between the cost of opening for longer and the potential sales upside has shifted as costs have risen. Do opening hours in every location match the footfall?

- Operating hours – many retail operations have people onsite for longer than the store is open, adding salary and heat, light and power costs. Bringing tasks from 'out of hours' operations into quiet parts of the day can reduce costs.

- As hourly costs rise, it is worth revisiting if tasks can be outsourced. For example, outsourcing cash counting and banking could be a more cost-effective way of cash accounting. And there may be things you can 'outsource' to a central team, such as phone calls.

- Many businesses control costs by managing their investment profile. That can be holding back on when a big investment is made, or it can be a more local holding back on filling vacancies – especially if they are aware of an upcoming change that will reduce required resource levels.

be a more level holding and increase the depth of overall strategy of merge of an upcoming fracture attempt to its required openness is to.

Chapter 4

How do I balance investing in sales and controlling costs?

The bedrock of business success is spotting an opportunity and investing in it. There are the exciting stories of people mortgaging their homes for the last roll of the dice for a business venture that finally comes good. Less excitingly, it is businesses who consistently balance their books and carve out a budget to seed future growth that delivers the predictable returns that investors love.

The reality is that investing to grow sales requires money, whether that is to hire more sales people, buy a tech solution to transform customer experience or to put effort into developing new products and services.

Unless your business has unlimited cash reserves, new money to fund a growth project will have to be found from somewhere. Anyone who has worked in a large organisation will be familiar with the annual round of budget submissions and trade-off discussions that happen so that senior leaders can be sure they are making the best investment decisions with the available funds.

If you are investing in new projects and have to hold the cost line steady, savings will have to be found from business as usual. So how do you find the money for growth? It brings us back to the eternal productivity challenge of striving to reduce downtime and minimising time spent on tasks to free up more resources to spend on things customers value and drive sales.

This chapter is a bit like the business equivalent of looking for a few stray coins down the back of the sofa or rummaging for some loose change in the depths of your handbag. You will probably need to find more than a handful of loose change before you are be able to free up investment money without impacting your operation, but it is possible especially if you know the right places to look. Let's find out how.

First of all, you need to know where the money spent on your operation really goes. Just like at home if you need to economise, all the advice is to understand your regular outgoings and then make decisions on where to trim costs. In business it can be hard to know exactly where the money goes. You probably know what the salary budget is at a total and individual level. And you can usually tell how much is spent on management and specialist roles. Beyond that, it is hard to be sure how much you are spending serving customers, moving stock or completing admin.

Remember in Chapter 2, we can improve our customer service by reducing process times and capitalising on marginal gains? And in Chapter 3 where we explore streamlining and making our resources work better for us to ensure we are reducing our costs? These concepts can also be used to find the money to invest back into the business.

What other activities can we reduce or eliminate altogether to make these savings?

The first is to find any tasks you can either stop doing or do less frequently to free up time and cost without affecting customers.

The good news is there are two great ways to free up cash for investment in an operation.

There are usually activities that teams have done for years which have become an organisational comfort blanket as they have weaved themselves deep into the fabric of how the business works. They become habits that everyone relies on without considering if it is an activity that serves us well anymore. A typical comfort blanket is doing a lot of stock counts in the belief that we are managing stock really well. Or a problem happens once and a series of steps are put in place so we don't have to worry about it ever happening again, even if the risk is low. Or it can simply be that the processes you put in place to get you to where you are now, are not needed for where you are going next.

Do you have habitual processes that don't serve you well anymore? You can tell if you have spotted one because if you suggest changing it, there will be a collective gasp and silence while people contemplate all the things that might possibly go wrong if you stopped doing it. It's those processes which colleagues have an emotional attachment to but are no longer the result of cold, hard, business logic that are the ones to review. They can be so engrained that even if head office says to stop the process, operations teams can't quite bring themselves to believe everything will be okay if they just stop. Change management is needed to make it stick!

What are these incredible processes that cast such a spell over an organisation? Examples include:

- line by line checking of deliveries from internal warehouses – in the grand scheme of things, it doesn't matter if your delivery is a couple of boxes short if it is still within the company ownership.

- Counting stock over and over again – humans make errors and less frequent counting leads to more accurate stock figures. You don't need to count everything, just do counts by exception – if you are getting close to having a gap that will affect customer experience and sales, or are starting to get a build up of a line, it means something has gone wrong and a counting intervention will help put it right. Routine cycle counting is at best an expensive comfort blanket and at worst, a way to make your stock file number less accurate with every human intervention.

- Excessive cashing up – does this need to be done every day? Or even after every colleague shift as some businesses do. As long as cash outturns stay within tight limits, less is more. Especially in today's society where cash payments are in continual decline.

- Audits and compliance checks – these have a habit of starting as a tight list of essentials and evolve to become a huge list of checks covering everything that anyone worries about. Over time the list grows and can easily become disconnected from meaningful analysis of business risk, becoming the ultimate comfort blanket. Some checks have to be done and are essential for safe and legal operation of the business. Does your audit list include things that go beyond the essential? Are there things that operations teams do just to make sure they don't fail an audit that don't really add any value anymore?

- Meetings and conference calls – for one monthly team meeting, I confess I took in work I had saved specifically so I could get some benefit from the day. Do you have meetings and calls that are part of that organisational security blanket rather than adding value? What could you do if you released your leaders' time and used it in a different way?

Has any of this list made you feel uncomfortable? If so, follow that discomfort, it is telling you where to look to free up some time in your business.

The second place to look is in your customer-facing tasks. It might make you feel uncomfortable again as customer-facing time is where your brand magic happens, when you really drive sales and is how you create your loyal customer base that supports your success, isn't it?

Yes. Customer time is all those things and they are really important. Yet if you have a deep dive look at how you spend time with customers, you will probably find things that neither you or your customer value, yet take both your time. You can spot them as they are often the times when the customer is hanging around and waiting while the colleague is doing something else. As a customer, you will have spotted these potential time savers in other businesses. Yet once it is your process and you know what the colleagues are doing and why, it becomes harder to find opportunities to speed up customer interactions. Creating possible solutions to speed up customer work is the point where efficiency and customer experience experts combine their interests. You are searching for the win-win that improves customer journeys and saves you time too.

You might have experienced some of the examples on the next page as a customer, and could use them to reflect on the possibilities to improve your own customer processes.

- Colleagues searching for your order when you go to pick it up – an online order, a prescription, your new glasses, the dry cleaning. It feels like it's part of the time serving the customer, yet the customer is often left hanging around while the process is inefficient.

- Slow systems and excessive data input, meaning customers spend time looking at the top of a colleague's head while drumming their fingers on the desk – checking in to hotels; some loyalty schemes that require an email to be entered; car hire pick up. Most times, orders are placed on anything other than a custom designed app.

- Self-check-out tills that throw up constant colleague intervention requests and slow the process – such as weight-check bagging areas that can't cope with light items like greeting cards and small items of clothing, to missing barcodes, price reduction tickets that won't scan and marketing vouchers that need colleague input. You will have experienced this and more while shopping. How many happen at your tills?

You can quantify the opportunity to eliminate this non-customer-friendly time from your process by measuring how long customer interactions take using work study, which is also known as 'time and motion' study. By breaking down the overall customer interaction into smaller steps, you can see how long each bit takes and easily isolate the parts that don't add value.

For example, the average time taken for a customer to go to a counter and ask for their online order to them getting it in their hands is one and half minutes. The vast majority of that time is the customer waiting with no one talking to them as a colleague walks to find their order, rummages through a distant storage area and walks back. We've seen plenty of instances that take much longer than ninety seconds; to the point where it would be faster for the customer to select their products off the shelf and pay through a till. We've also seen slick processes with parcel storage close to hand that have customers on their way with their parcel in under thirty seconds.

The case studies overleaf give examples of businesses who have measured their processes and found ways to speed up their customer facing processes in a way that works for them and their customers.

By breaking down the overall customer interaction into smaller steps, you can see how long each bit takes and easily isolate the parts that don't add value.

Case Studies - How others have freed up time for growth.

Business have used work study to deep dive their customer facing process and take away their process checking comfort blankets.

Example 1:

A fashion accessories business relies on great sales people to ensure browsers become buyers and then drive extra value by selling additional items or trading customers up to their premium products. Alongside the great sales work they do, they add customer details to their customer database for future marketing by asking for an email address. A newly introduced loyalty scheme was not integrated into their systems effectively, so they were asking the customer to repeat their email to register with the loyalty scheme, adding an extra minute every time they serve a customer. By resolving the problem the retailer removed duplicated admin and helped their colleagues focus on closing the sale.

Example 2:

WHSmith is an example of a retailer who drives extra sales by asking every customer if they would like to buy the chocolate bar of the week at the side of the till. Some retailers go further and ask if you found everything you wanted; promote offers of the day; suggest loyalty card sign ups, bag for life purchases and more. Done well, it can feel natural and engaging to a customer and adds to sales. Done badly, it becomes a robotic series of questions that just wastes time for customers and colleagues alike.

Example 3:

A fashion retailer cashed up each till drawer as soon as a colleague moved off it to try and reduce the risk of theft from colleagues. This not only kept team leaders busy counting cash rather than being available for customers and their teams, it meant tills were out of action at key times. Shift changeovers meant that some till points were closed while customer queues got longer and colleagues waited to start work until a freshly counted till was available. Is the theft reduction benefit outweighing time taken on counts and customer walk outs when queues build and don't move fast enough? It also had a demoralising effect on their staff. This often can lead to an unmotivated workforce, negatively impacting sales.

Example 4:

A retailer had successfully transformed their operation and moved from a business with the dreaded combination of too much of the wrong stock, gaps on shelves that led to missed sales and broken processes to a fantastic operation with great compliance. To make this amazing change happen, the business had put in places ways of working that were designed to fix the problems and double check compliance. Even though their stores were now running well, they had retained all the extra processes that were needed to fix their old problems. They hadn't switched to the sort of slimmed down processes that are more suited to keeping a well run operation ticking along. The extra work in counting stock, compliance checking and maintaining extra trackers was adding about 10% more activity in to the store than was needed. Having seen the success that those double checking processes had brought, it felt a scary step to take some of them away. The easy bit was identifying what they didn't need to do anymore, the more difficult bit was persuading an organisation that they wouldn't go back to their old problems if they carefully peeled away the extra processes.

So much of the work required to deliver productivity improvement relies on effective change management.

Quick Wins – What can I do now?

Some change is difficult to deliver. The good news is that if you can spot ways to reduce pain points for both customers and colleagues, you will be onto a quick win.

● Ask your teams what they think takes unnecessary time and slows them down when looking after customers. They are the experts in spotting the frustration of things not working right, over-elaborate processes and activities that just seem plain pointless.

● Many brands recognise the value of direct customer feedback and have put in place customer experience programmes to put customer insight at the heart of their operation. If you have experience data in your organisation already, use it to identify things that are frustrating for customers. If you eliminate customer frustrations you will be growing your business and saving your team's time too.

● Watch customer interactions in your business – when is the customer waiting while the colleague does something, or their time is taken with something that can be sped up or even stopped?

● Look at any checklists and audits managers have to do and consider if they are really needed? Fear of the consequences of failing an audit can drive creation of a culture where everything is double checked beyond where it is adding value.

There is an urgency to freeing up resources to invest in growth. Businesses not investing in moving forward are actually moving backwards compared to their proactive competitors. Search hard for your own quick wins and take the approach originating from Silicon Valley start-ups of failing early and fast so you test, learn, and move forward quickly.

The bigger the emotional attachment to the old ways of doing things, the bigger the change challenge is.

Chapter 5:

Is my leadership structure right?

Leaders matter. Having the right local leadership model determines business success and shapes customer and colleague experience. Anyone who has held a multi-site leadership role, such as an area or regional manager, knows the difference between a good operation and a great one is the local leader and how they go about their role. It's an endless challenge to find enough great managers for each of your sites, while providing people with the right degree of stretch and growth opportunities to fulfil their potential.

Great leaders have teams that enjoy working for them and employee turnover levels are lower as colleagues value the experience of working for a good boss – an important factor in today's tight labour markets where juggling vacancies is an ongoing operational challenge in many businesses.

Besides recruiting, retaining and developing great people, businesses also must make sure they have a framework that leaders can operate in. Sometimes referred to as the rather fancy-sounding organisational design, it means having the right number and mix of leadership roles to deliver everything needed for a smooth-running operation, supported colleagues and happy customers .

Going back thirty years or more, businesses tended to be hierarchical with many layers between the workers and the ultimate boss. Society and business have changed, and layers have been removed to create flatter organisations with fewer departmental and deputy managers. Some businesses even have leaderless, self-managed teams, although this tends to work best in situations where a group of established experts work cross functionally, such as in creative industries, for example.

Customer-facing businesses have tended to retain local leaders. In part because customers expect to be able to call on a manager to resolve any problems that arise, and because there are legal and safety requirements that are often best delivered with the clear accountability that a unit manager brings.

How many management roles and different levels do you need? There is no simple, correct answer that works for all organisations. It depends on what your business is trying to deliver for your customers and teams. However, there are some guiding principles to follow to set you up for success.

What is the ideal local leadership structure for your business?

- How are local sites contributing to how you deliver your overall business strategy? What is their role and how should they go about it? For example, if you are selling premium products or services, you might want leadership roles that are sales coaches with a focus on training and people management. If you are a discount outlet, you will want the minimum management cover to deliver an efficient, lower cost operation.

- Are you clear on what the purpose of each role is? How should they be spending time? How should time be split between supervising the operation, ensuring compliance and coaching teams?

- Each leadership role should be differentiated from any others, so it has its own unique reason for being. For example, if you have a deputy manager and a senior supervisor role, what is the difference between the roles, other than a pay band? If they do broadly the same thing, do you need the complexity of two roles?

- How well understood are the roles? There should be consistency in how a given role spends their time across different locations. Lack of role clarity creates variation between sites. Variation tends to increase over time and leads to a variable employee and customer experience too.

- How much time do your leaders spend leading versus doing things that others can do? When higher paid management roles complete a lot of general tasks, you end up spending a higher hourly rate for work that others could do just as well for a lower cost. Imagine you have four supervisors on a shift each spending half their time doing general tasks that anyone can do, are that many supervisors needed?

- Consider how the structure you have encourages development, offers career progression and allows you to develop your own talent. For example, if no stores have deputy managers, is there a route from team leader to manager without the jump being too big?

Your structure design requires a balance of all the aspects above to have a structure that delivers for you, your people and your customers. Business, colleague and customer expectations change over time, so the structure that was perfect just five years ago might not be serving you as well now. As happens in life and business, things keep changing and all aspects of the operation benefit from ongoing review.

Without a good grounding in facts, decisions about changing structures can be subjective, based on old and out of date experiences of the roles being reviewed, as well as being downright emotive. Adding in the facts balances the feelings. Measuring how leaders spend their time creates a sound evidence base on which to make structural decisions.

How do I know if I've got my leadership structure right?

To quote the title of 80s singer songwriter, Joe Jackson's best-selling record, "You Can't Get What You Want, (Till You Know What You Want)". A business conversation is required to define what you want your leadership structure to deliver. It's not just about cost, although that will probably be a consideration, it's about how you deliver customer and colleague experience to two of the groups that matter most. So a good place to start is with some simple guiding principles that you can stack up both today's and any future structures against.

Do you want the role to be part of the operation, working alongside the team delivering the day to day? Is it a more strategic business leadership role with accountability for key elements of the profit and loss report? Do you want your leaders to be office based or where the operational action is? Looking across your operation, are they all the same or do bigger operations need a bigger leadership team?

An important consideration is how you see the manager's interaction with their team. Most businesses say they want their local managers to adopt a coaching style, providing a mix of support, stretch and feedback to create a high performing team.

Dulcie Swanston's excellent book, *It's Not Bloody Rocket Science* sets out a model for leadership behaviour that creates high performing teams and individuals. Based on neuroscience and psychology, the book provides a framework that balances stretch and support for individual growth and performance through the quality of conversations that happen throughout the day (Top Right Thinking)[2].

To create evidence examining the current structure to form a basis for decision making, the gold standard is to measure how different leadership roles spend their time. A work study analyst shadowing roles for a period of their working day or week, measured across different sites, creates a robust picture of how time is spent.

Crucially, it also shows what gets in the way of leaders spending more time with their teams and customers.

By overlaying Dulcie's Top Right Thinking model, we can go further than measuring what leaders are doing and measure the *quality* of conversations they are having with their teams too. This is important because it tells us much more about the leadership

---

2 At ReThink, we've worked with Dulcie to create a way to measure the quality of leadership conversations that we've put into practice with a number of clients. The outputs are always illuminating and provide hard evidence of what we all instinctively know, that how our boss interacts with us affects how we work.

style that has developed over time in the business, the experience of colleagues, and the effectiveness of leadership training.

We've seen a colleague spoken to harshly by their manager where the stretch and challenge far outweighed the support provided. As a result, that colleague's performance was negatively impacted. They worked at a much slower pace for a long period until they eventually bounced back to their usual self. We measured the impact of that leader's conversation, and we think it's a safe bet to say that colleague felt pretty unhappy about the interaction with their manager that morning and probably didn't enjoy being at work. On the flip side, it's easy to see why having regular conversations, knowing you can trust your manager to be supportive while challenging you to do your best, creates an enjoyable place to work.

The aim of onsite role measurement is to create a fact base and to surface insights informing your decision making when considering leadership structures.

1. How should each role be spending their time?

It is often a surprise to know how much time is taken up with admin and emails. Is the manager in the office or with the team? How long is spent in meetings or Zoom calls? What extra work do area managers ask local leaders to do? How much time is spent on compliance checks and audits? Do team huddles happen regularly?

All these questions and more are answered from a look at how time is split by task for leadership roles. Mostly it delivers results that are surprising to central teams. There is always an aspect of manager workload that takes way more time than anyone expected. This type of study also highlights whether managers have the tools they need for the job. Slow running systems, Wi-Fi issues – and even the tasks that managers take home because they need somewhere without interruptions to focus on them – are all logged and the impact quantified.

Manager's time

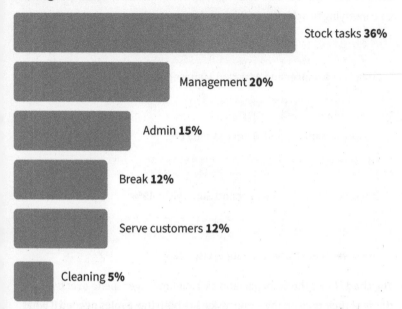

Stock tasks **36%**

Management **20%**

Admin **15%**

Break **12%**

Serve customers **12%**

Cleaning **5%**

2. Are roles differentiated?

Looking at data from different leadership roles in the same business allows us to quantify the degree of overlap in how time is spent between roles. There will always be some overlap between roles as there are generic and general tasks to be completed. If the crossover is 80% of their time spent doing the same things, is the remaining 20% really different enough to justify having two separate roles? In most cases, businesses decide it isn't. We commonly see high crossover between the site manager and their deputy. If this is because the site operates long hours and they work on mainly opposite shifts, the high crossover is a good thing as it suggests consistent leadership for teams. If they work largely the same hours and work on shift together, does it add value having two roles doing essentially the same thing?

Similarly, we often see high crossover when there are both supervisor and team leader roles in a structure. Are they really different roles? Are both needed?

In most cases there are no clear right or wrong answers, it all depends what you are trying to achieve.

Crossover Manager and Assistant Manager **68%**

Crossover Manager and Team Leader **31%**

Crossover Assistant Manager and Supervisor **49%**

Crossover Team leader and Supervisor **78%**

The chart shows the manager and assistant manager spend over two thirds of their time on the same tasks. Are both these roles needed if what they do is so similar?

Similarly, there is a high degree of task crossover between the team leader and supervisor. This suggests the business could drop from having four different management roles to just three and create differentiated roles with clear accountabilities.

In most businesses, more than three leadership levels suggest an opportunity to simplify the structure without impacting career paths.

3. Are roles consistent across different sites?

Consistency matters for lots of reasons. A team manager in one place paid the same as team managers somewhere else, would probably become dissatisfied or even feel taken advantage of if they were routinely expected to take on more responsibility than others doing the same role. Conversely, a team manager who never had a chance to get involved in wider leadership discussions while all the others did, may well feel that they were missing out.

If you want your people to be able to work flexibly and move between sites, roles need to be consistent for those people swaps to feel smooth and easy for all concerned.

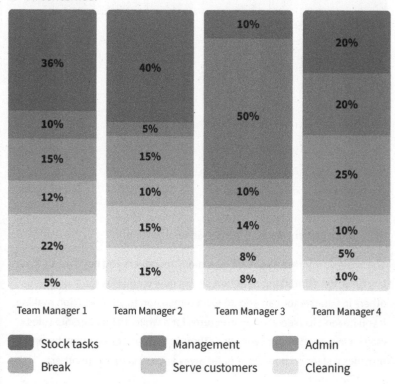

The answer to role inconsistency is usually role clarification, whether linked to a structure change or not.

4. How much management time versus general time?

Time on management does matter for the individual role holder and the business. If as a supervisor, you get little time to do anything other than the tasks that everyone else can do, you might feel unable to use your talents to best effect and look for a similar role elsewhere that allows you to spread your wings. For the business, if your leaders all spend more than half their time doing general tasks, you have many of your core tasks being done at a high hourly rate.

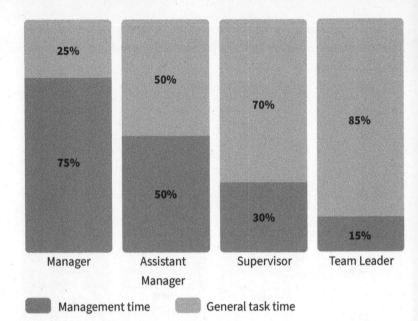

25%	50%	70%	85%
75%	50%	30%	15%
Manager	Assistant Manager	Supervisor	Team Leader

Management time   **General task time**

The analysis informs a view on how many managers you need on shift at any time. Benchmarking data that shows how your roles stack up versus others in your sector can add an extra dimension to your decision making. If you haven't looked at your structures for a while, the leadership roles may have moved out of sync with others in your sector and benchmarking provides a steer on how close or far away your structure is to others.

This technique of shadowing a specific role for a day or week can also be applied to specialist roles. For any role paid a premium to complete a specific task, understanding how much time they spend on the things that only they are uniquely qualified for versus doing things others can do is a key measure of how effectively that specialist resource is deployed. Generally, focusing a specialist on their specialty adds most value for the organisation.

The ability to focus on specialist roles makes it a useful technique in service industries, office environments, healthcare settings and more Getting the most from your top talent is always a valuable aim to pursue.

Case Studies - How others have focused on their leaders.

Role insight has helped other organisations make the most of their specialist and leadership roles.

Example 1:

Role study of department heads within a large retail business showed that many of their leaders were pulled into operational tasks rather than having time for their teams. The exception was the department head of a newly established team for home deliveries, who was spending more time with their team. Observations showed that they used the live progress tracking tools they were provided with to coach their team to meet the deadlines. For example, if a colleague's pick rate dropped one morning, live data showed the decline in performance as it was happening, so the department head could check in and support the colleague. The difference between leaders in the same store showed the power of real-time operational Key Performance Indicators (KPIs) and how data helped managers adopt a person led approach to their leadership.

Example 2:

A study of a specialist sales role looked at how different salespeople split their time over the week. Some role holders kept Monday free as their admin day and aimed to be out with potential clients the rest of the week. It was seen as sensible diary planning until the study showed that salespeople who were out every day and kept some time for their admin at the start and end of the day spent more time with customers overall. They also produced proposals and pricing information for new deals in a more timely manner than their once a week admin counterparts. The admin becomes a big chore that needs a dedicated chunk of time if you let it build up, but tackling it as it arises actually frees up more time for selling. It was an insight that was obvious once it showed up in the data – of course it must be better to be out selling every day. Many sales orientated businesses still have an admin day, along with the risk that once a set chunk of time has been carved out, the admin work expands to fill that time.

Example 3:

A hospitality business was focussing on upskilling their leaders so they could both provide the best working environment for colleagues and retain the best talent. They were deploying the Top Right Thinking model and were using work study observations to measure the conversation quality to track improvements – and prove the link between better quality leadership conversations of their management roles. As well as creating a base line for later comparison, the role study also highlighted several admin tasks that managers were carrying out. Simplifying, automating and removing as many of these as possible would free up time to carry out even more high-quality conversations.

Example 4:

Studying specialist roles in a clinical environment showed that highly trained individuals were often drawn into completing some of the more general tasks that needed to be done – such as mopping floors, laundry tasks and routine admin. Freeing up specialists from work that could be successfully completed by a lower paid role created more capacity for appointments.

Quick wins: What you can do for your organisational roles.

Organisational changes or alterations in how specialists are deployed are best made using data. However, there are some indicators that a change might be overdue without the benefit of work study data.

- How many reporting levels are there in the business? If there are more than three, there is an opportunity to streamline the structure. Many businesses now operate on just two management levels. Adding in a deputy manager for your biggest businesses, for example, can also create more career path and development opportunities within the business than a very flat structure would provide.

- Reviewing job specifications – are they clear and do they show the unique requirements of each role? Where there is role overlap, there can be an opportunity to review if all the overlapping roles are needed and how many of each role you need at any one time.

- If you have field or client-based teams, how much geographical overlap is there? Do you have colleagues driving past each other at the expense of company time and the planet's resources when a redrawing of boundaries would save time?

If the differences between roles is a bit blurry on paper, you can guarantee it is also blurry in real life.

- Got a leadership or specialist role vacancy? Can you use it to test out a new structure or way of working? Keep your experiments time bound so your business retains a consistent way of doing things and use vacancies as a chance to learn what could happen if you did things differently.

Chapter 6:

What can we stop doing to free up our people?

In a world where businesses are looking to differentiate themselves and add more value for customers, bringing in new services and customer offer elements are usually in the mix. This means business operations are getting evermore complex.

If your business has bottomless salary budgets and can recruit great candidates in a currently tight labour market, then you can just keep adding more things to do and more people to do them.

Is anyone's business like that? The reality is that most businesses want to stop doing things that don't add value for customers, not just because it's a sensible way to work but because it frees up resources to pursue their strategic agenda. Whether that is adding in new services such as home delivery, upselling customers and collecting emails to grow their customer database, or moving to be more consultative rather than transactional;

stopping doing something else is what creates the capacity for growth into new areas.

Stopping doing things is a great story for your teams too. Most people work hard to fit in everything they need to do, and just piling in new work is demoralising. It's easy to lose control of priorities once there's just too much to do, and people decide for themselves what to keep on their to-do list and what tasks they won't get round to. A clear story of the tasks you are removing and how the time can be better used provides a great basis to manage change and deliver a consistent implementation.

It sounds like it should be easy to stop doing things. It should be simple, right? Yet it will take more effort than you might expect for your team to believe that it is okay to stop doing that thing you've asked them to do for the last ten years. Especially if you'd linked it to performance-related pay, a bonus scheme or an audit process in the past. People can take some convincing that something that was important for so long really is no longer needed. You'll need to clearly explain why it is okay to stop the task – and probably more than once. Your team want to do a good job and stopping activities takes at least as much change management effort as starting something new.

Finding things to stop doing.

The best things to stop doing are:

- activities that do not directly impact how customers experience your services

- tasks that are not absolutely essential for how the business operates.

Spotting tasks you can just stop doing should be the easy part, but it can be surprisingly difficult. The tricky bit is stepping back from the operation to find things that you have done for years where the time spent outweighs any benefit. The best candidates for stopping are those tasks that have been put in place with good intentions, that might even have been necessary at the time and have become deeply ingrained habits, yet no longer serve any good purpose.

Easy targets for things to stop doing are any checklists, audits, papers and records that have to be stored for a period of time. Audits, in particular, are put in place to manage a potential risk and come weighed down with dire consequences if audits are failed. But is everything on the list still needed? What if you stopped the ones that aren't a legal requirement? Are some audit tasks just an expensive comfort blanket or is it really addressing a genuine risk for your business?

It's a common occurrence that when new systems and processes are implemented, the audit list is not updated at the same time. It's easy for old checks to stay on the audit list, even if the risk they are there to manage is wiped out by a new way of doing things.

Next place to look is in the office and see how many folders, files and logbooks are in there. Many of them can be got rid of with associated time saved too.

It's not just about getting rid of paper folders. Any admin completed is ripe for a reality check, even if it is done on a smart app. And especially if it is a tracker that is completed on a laptop, saved and then emailed to someone else to collate. Is it essential or just a nice to do? If it goes to head office, does someone there really need it? Or even do anything with it?

Looking at admin and audits is symbolically important as well as being a good practical step too. Reducing admin usually frees up management time, so it supports senior leadership messages on business priorities and finding time for new initiatives.

In most businesses stopping non-essential admin can free up some office time, but it won't save a big chunk of time across the whole team. For that you must look at the core work the team does. It varies by business. In retail it is usually stock processes; in food outlets it is making high volume food items; in warehouses it is travel time while picking orders; in office environments it is usually data management of one form or another.

Counting stock is time-consuming in most businesses. It feels like counting helps keep a tight control on your stock, yet the opposite is true in most cases. It's not surprising when you think how difficult we make it.

> **The reality is that humans aren't very good at counting stock and tend to make mistakes.**

The same stock might be in three or four places in a shop – the stock room, the normal shelf, a promotion end, next to the checkouts etc. Adding interruptions from customers and colleagues, with perhaps less than ideal kit to do the counts, and counting without ever making a mistake starts to look more like the difficult challenge it really is.

Knowing how much retail stock you have is essential if you are going to make sure that both customers in store and online will be able to buy the items they want from you. Most retailers have a digital log of where they think their stock is – a theoretical stock file. And how close the theory is to reality can vary significantly. For other businesses it's about knowing how many raw ingredients, packaging materials and manufacturing components you have on hand.

Tests have shown that over time, the more often stock is counted, the bigger the difference between reality and theoretical number becomes. Counting errors compound every time the stock is counted, so the actual value of stock drifts further from the theoretical stock file number. What this means is retail customers face empty shelves when the business thinks stock levels are fine, and unexpected stockpiles build up where they are not needed. The answer isn't to count everything all the time. It is to look for these exceptions that show the stock figure has drifted. Most stores have a process for spotting gaps on the shelves and correcting the stock file number so more stock flows back in. Smart retailers do minimal, targeted counts and save the many hours of work it would take to count everything.

It's the same for any business that needs to know what supplies are available and where they are at any one time. Tech can help with many businesses using RFID to keep a track of exactly where their supplies are. RFID relies on stock items carrying a unique tag that emits a radio frequency that can be picked up by a receiver beacon. The tag and beacon can tell you which part of a building the stock is in, a bit like using the 'Find My' app on your phone. The system maintains a constant balance of stock holding so there is no need to count and no human error distorting the numbers.

Your core processes feel like the most difficult to tackle yet will deliver you the highest rewards. And if you have a process improvement team within your business, this is where you'd want them to focus the majority of their time and attention.

Case Studies – What other businesses have stopped doing.

Examples range from things that affect the time of just one person in the team to changes that free up many hours a week:

Example 1:

Customers use cards rather than cash these days, so volumes of cash taken in most retail businesses have been slashed. Years ago, busy retailers at Christmas took so many banknotes and coins they needed to empty tills throughout the day. Literally, piles of cash were counted and banked. Along with that there were all the paper cheques and slips from credit card transactions to deal with that have now become distant memories for some and ancient history for most.

Now, most payment is electronic and cash bundles are small. Yet many businesses still cash up every till every day. They balance the float in each till, count the cash taken and count everything in the safe too – even bags that were already counted and security sealed yesterday in some cases. Unless there is an active theft situation where money is going missing, cashing up once a week saves a significant chunk of managers' time and

Technology can help free up time from cashing up too.

is frequent enough to keep track of the cash you are taking. Some retailers use clever banknote caches that count the money as the notes are posted into the box, and the most recent self-checkout tills are also self-cashing up tills. Other retailers just scoop the cash from the tills into bank bags and the bank count the money for them in huge, automated, high security centres. And when you do a manual till count, use scales to weigh coins and save you time.

Cash management is usually completed as a two-person job to reduce the risk of loss, so reducing cashing up frequency to once a week usually saves about an hour of team time every day.

Example 2:

Businesses using fridges have to monitor and record the temperatures every day to make sure that sensitive food items and medicines are held at the correct temperature to keep them safe and effective to use. Many businesses have a scruffy looking paper log that is filled in and signed each day. Smart fridges monitor their own temperatures and have an alarm that lets the team know if the temperature moves outside the tight safe range and create their own temperature log. It sounds a small thing yet consider how many fridges and freezers there are in a supermarket – and there are more than a customer sees in the warehouse too.

Other businesses that must check fire doors or do other audits daily are increasingly moving from paper trackers to tablet based tech. Moving to tablets is the perfect opportunity to check if the regular audit really is needed. And a big benefit is that information can be checked by an auditor remotely, rather than having someone come and look at a paper tracker.

Automated auditing doesn't just save time, it also ensures consistent compliance providing reassurance that things are running as they should to keep colleagues and customers safe.

Example 3:

Some businesses check off every item that comes into store on a delivery against a paper delivery note. Sounds sensible to make sure you receive the stock you are charged for, doesn't it? What if that stock is coming from your own warehouse, so any imbalance is within the company rather than a real business loss. Does the time and money spent checking deliveries seem sensible now?

Businesses that have stopped checking internal deliveries include a DIY retailer that received pallet loads of stock at a time, to a jewellery business receiving a small box that contained thousands of tiny items. It saves hours of work and means supplies get to where they are needed without the time delay that checking everything off entails.

If stock is coming directly from the supplier, you might want to check it versus what you are expecting the first time it hits your company. Some big businesses and suppliers want to avoid the workload and hassle of both sides checking deliveries and raising claims, so agree an average margin adjustment to manage the financial risk and save them both the work.

Example 4:

A DIY retailer completed routine stock counts of every item in the store over a two-month period. An enormous task in a big shop containing over 10,000 lines. Switching to exception counting of gaps and overstocks as they built up saved them a time equivalent of two people a week in every store.

Example 5:

An office-based service provider had to move data between spreadsheets. Data movements are most efficiently and accurately achieved when the data flow is automated. The manual processes this team used involved cutting and pasting numbers, and errors occurred when data was inadvertently pasted to the wrong line. Having identified where data transfers were needed, they worked with their IT counterparts to create the connections that automated the data movements. Another business routinely used Excel as part of their workflows, yet the team were not trained on the many basic Excel short cuts that could save them time. Adding Excel short cuts to their induction training helped establish a baseline of higher capability with core tools.

Quick Wins – What you can stop doing today.

STOCK

● Improve your stock figure accuracy and save time by stopping routine counts. Whether you call them perpetual inventory, counts, stock checks; put down the pen and paper or the handheld terminal and start saving time.

● If your stock file figures go negative it means you have more stock on hand than the system thinks you have. Your first reaction might be to count the line to get the stock level right. Let the system auto correct negative lines to zero so the system will reorder it and make sure it is in stock when it's needed.

CASH

● If it's not the right time for you to be investing in tech to minimise cash accounting time, why not outsource your cash counting? Just take the excess cash from the tills and safe, seal it in a bag and let a supplier count it for you and save your time.

● If you cash up every day, move to cashing up and safe reconciliations just once a week.

PAPER

- Go on a paper tracker hunt and when you find one, decide if you can stop it or automate it. Most businesses have more paper-based logs, trackers and audit sheets than you might imagine. Streamline and automate them to save time and improve compliance too.

AUDITS and DATA

- Review all the audits the team have to do. Is the risk the audit task is designed to address still important? Is the time spent minimising the risk proportionate? You might need to work with your internal audit teams to agree changes. If you do have to keep doing it, can it be automated? Or the frequency reduced?

- Any time you are taking data from one system to enter it into another – automate it.

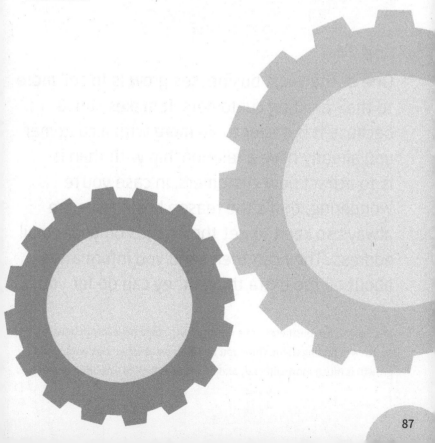

Chapter 7

I've added new services, how can I make them more efficient?

One of the ways businesses grow is to sell more to their existing customers. It makes sense because it is easier to do more with a customer you already have a relationship with than it is to attract new customers. In case you're wondering, that's the reason businesses are always so keen to get their hands on your email address. They can then send you information about all the extra things they can do for you.

Successful new businesses in a rapid growth stage have lots of new customers finding them. Once you're a well-established business, rapid growth is much more difficult, and businesses look to extend their services to keep growing. Examples of retailer service extensions include offering multichannel options such as click and collect and home delivery or moving from purely selling products to offering related services, such as: mobile phones at Tesco, vitamin testing in Holland & Barrett and car lightbulb replacement in Halfords. The same principle is at work in the service sector too. Your car insurer will offer you home insurance; your travel agent wants you to get your travel money and airport parking with them; the gas repair man wants to sell you boiler breakdown insurance. The list is endless and when the added services are a good fit, it can work well for customers and the company.

> **Even the milkman is looking to do more than supply your daily pint, offering other products alongside the core dairy range.**

It can be difficult to move into a new product or service area that you have no operational experience in. Rather than go through the pain of implementing a new service yourself, you can pair up with an existing supplier who already knows how to turn a profit. Perhaps one with good brand awareness? That's why Next have partnered with Costa and supermarkets have Starbucks in them rather than trying to learn how to make great coffee at speed themselves.

The challenge with starting anything new is it takes a while to get really efficient at it. There is an experience curve to climb and as you do more, you'll identify multiple ways to tweak and improve what you do and how you do it. Most new services start small, so it takes a while to have the volume that drives the improvement learning. Low, inconsistent volumes across multiple sites don't make it easy to learn quickly, yet it is the way many new services start.

An exception to the slow start rule was the private Covid-19 testing services that sprang up to meet the requirements for pretravel Covid testing. They did not have the usual slow, gradual start and they had to deal with the challenge of finding time to review how they were doing things while running at full capacity.

Another challenge for new services is they don't often start out with optimum systems. It's either not worth putting the investment into the ideal solution until you've tested the demand, or the system development takes longer than the rest of the start-up will, so become a later addition.

Businesses put a lot of effort into designing and launching new services. It's exciting work creating a new solution for a customer need. Yet there is so much to learn. Once the service launches, the hard work starts to test and learn, tweak and improve how the service runs for peak productivity and customer experience.

The principles of optimising a new service are broadly the same as those for improving the efficiency of well-established processes. Yet there are some productivity tools and techniques that can be particularly useful to accelerate the test and learn cycle.

How can you learn faster?

The same productivity principles apply to improving new processes. You want to work out how to do it faster, better and consistently. The difference is you are starting something new, so you probably don't have the same depth of experience to call on in your organisation and you might have a short timeline to prove it can work.

There are time and motion study techniques that dive into the fine detail of a process to help accelerate your learning and ascend the experience curve much faster. The trick with new processes is to escape the average trajectory and kick up performance to drive revenue faster and higher than you would otherwise have done.

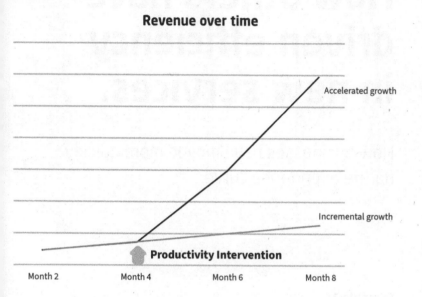

Revenue over time

Accelerated growth

Incremental growth

Productivity Intervention

Month 2   Month 4   Month 6   Month 8

Either a technique that breaks down processes into each individual movement allows you to quickly spot bottle necks and quantify opportunities to make things more efficient. Going through short test, learn, do cycles is a tried and tested way to embed learning and best practice into how you do things. This cycle helps you pin down that one best way to do things, meaning you can train your teams the most efficient way right from the start.

This sort of time and motion work uses short, sharp study techniques that create insights that focus efforts where they make the most difference.

Case Studies – How others have driven efficiency in new services.

How businesses have moved more quickly up the experience curve.

Example 1:

A retailer streamlined their stock management process and used systems to make sure stores only received price and recall notifications for stock they actually had in store, saving stores time and paper, no longer having to wade through reams of paper to check for the lines they hold. Work study identified additional processes that the principles could easily be extended to, relating to promotion implementation and essential stock counts. This increased the benefits they achieved from their process change and made life easier for store teams.

Example 2:

A grocery store started to offer quick service home delivery direct from the local store. This is something many stores have done as the Deliveroo style delivery principle has been extended from just takeaway food to groceries on demand. Retailers launching these services find delivery requests coming at all times of day – from customers ordering booze and snacks in the evening, to cereal and cigarettes in the morning.

Grocery stores are good at taking things from a delivery and putting them on the shelves. A delivery service requires a colleague to collect a prescribed list of items from the shelf and pack them up ready for delivery. It sounds like an easy reversal of what they currently do, yet it is quite a different process that relies heavily on technology and speed to make it cost effective. On demand grocery operations could learn efficiency lessons from warehouses where they are experts in picking stock from a huge inventory – it's just on a larger scale.

Studying the process from an order being received on a terminal to it being loaded to a delivery van showed multiple opportunities to speed up the process – meaning customers get their orders quicker and the service is more profitable. The biggest opportunity was picking the order directly to the delivery bag and scanning them as they went. Initially, teams were picking items into a basket or trolley, taking it to a till to process the sale and then separately packing the order for delivery. Picking and scanning direct to the delivery bag saved minutes for each order. Something those of us who use retailers' scan and pack technology understand when we do our own grocery shopping.

> **Sometimes when we start something new, we develop a blind spot to the obvious.**

Example 3:

A retailer introduced an extra shelf at the top of each display that was intended to hold extra stock that would not fit on the main shelf. The idea was that having surplus stock close to where it was needed would save time walking backwards and forwards between the stock room when more stock was needed. Making it easy to top up the shelves, stock would always be there when a customer wanted it. A small study in a handful of stores showed they had not implemented the extra storage in the same way. One store had done a great job and were saving lots of time versus their old way of working, proving that the cost of change would be quickly paid back. Extra stock was neatly stacked above its usual shelf and miles walked to the stockroom were eliminated. Another store was using the shelves but had just put the excess stock anywhere there was a free space rather than above the same stock on the shelf. This means that they just replaced walking to the stockroom and back with a wander round the shop, trying to spot where on a high shelf the stock they needed was. The study showed a different approach to communication would be needed to get the planned benefit.

Example 4:

A quick serve restaurant uses detailed work study timings so they know how long it takes to make every item on their menu, right down to the cost of adding a squirt of sauce or an extra slice of cheese. They use this information when creating new products because they know the labour cost of adding each ingredient. It allows them to make sophisticated flavour and cost decisions when it comes to creating their next promotion special – is that gherkin slice really necessary?

Quick Wins – What you can do on your own.

As discussed in previous chapters, work study will find opportunities to do things more efficiently that you won't find on your own, but that shouldn't stop you finding some of the easy to spot ones yourself before you bring in the specialists. Good places to start are:

- Spend time watching your people carry out a process. When does the movement of the team look less like a well-oiled machine and become more chaotic? The point when the smooth flow stops shows a process point that is worth a closer look.

- Visit when you are not expected, so you can see how things really are versus what you want to see. Go at the busiest time to see how processes hold up and at the quietest times to understand how your capacity at peak holds up against demand and what your labour cost profile looks like during quiet times.

- If a supplier has provided equipment to help you launch your service, use their know-how. Ask them to look over how you are working and give you pointers to improve what you do.

> **We went to study how a team was working with a new process and were asked if we wanted to see what head office had told them to do or what they really did!**

- Establish a good set of process KPIs so you know whether what you are doing will be profitable and if things are working as efficiently as expected.

- Ask the team what is working well and what is difficult. They will know when things are not easy and running smooth for them.

- Review your implementation guides and associated communication. Have you given the button pressing instructions or gone further so teams really know how to operate for peak efficiency? Clue: if it has just gone out via a written message in email or on the intranet, there is probably more you can do.

Growing your business by selling more to existing customers makes sense. It makes commercial sense to get as efficient with your new services as quickly as you can to ensure a good customer experience, make the change process easy for your teams and optimise your financial return.

Chapter 8

How do I find my next set of productivity improvements?

Developing the productivity of an operation is a journey, not an end point. Successful businesses don't operate like museum pieces stuck in time. They are dynamic and evolve with the everchanging competitive environment, customer preferences and commercial constraints.

Like all journeys, a map can help guide you to your destination. A productivity roadmap should set out your future improvement opportunities, and when and how you are going to get there. We are all used to using satnavs helping us get where we need to be and no longer rely on static maps. Updates on traffic flows and road conditions mean our satnavs refresh our route as we go. Your productivity roadmap needs to be as dynamic as a satnav so your route to productivity is amended as you learn from implementing changes and as the environment alters around you.

Being responsible for delivering productivity improvements means constantly evaluating where you are and resetting your course to identify and implement the next wave of changes. You might have smoothly landed a huge plan and smashed delivery of the value case. Then you'll find there is no time to sit around congratulating yourself. That saving was baked into the financial plans months ago and becomes history the second the project is completed. So it's on to the next stage of journey as you refine your roadmap and constantly scan the horizon for the next set of changes.

There is always a need to find more and new savings. National Living wage increases are pushing up salary costs, margins are being squeezed on all sides and the business wants to free up some cash to invest in new opportunities. So, it's time to go back round the cycle of identifying more opportunities and trading them off through the budgeting process again.

Even if there aren't pressing cost challenges, it just makes sense to finding the best way to do what you do – and that includes doing things as efficiently as you can.

Ideally you will already have a productivity roadmap, made up of a series of projects that deliver planned savings over different time scales. A steady flow of improvements that deliver savings is the ideal way to work. It's no good having a 'jam tomorrow' plan that solely relies on a big pay off in the future. Experience tells us that's a high-risk strategy which may not survive the constantly changing priorities of modern business. The best productivity roadmaps are made up of a set of projects and initiatives that deliver a series of benefits over different timeframes, a mix of short- and medium-term deliverables. To create and deliver this sort of plan requires a constant cycle of plan, do, and review. Plan then deliver an improvement, check the benefit delivery and then review where you are and identify the next set of improvement opportunities.

Even if you have the perfect plan, you can be sure the time will come when the business faces an extra challenge, and you are asked to find even more savings than you have identified in your plan. It's just the way business works.

So, whether you are starting from scratch or already have a brilliant plan yet your boss wants even more, where can you look?

Where can you find even more savings?

When identifying more savings for your roadmap plan, these are two good places to start looking:

1. Technology

Technology keeps improving and as it becomes more widely adopted, it tends to become more affordable too. This means there might be time-saving tech that you have previously looked at and discounted as not meeting the return levels you need, maybe the numbers stack up better this time. Or it could be the technology has gotten better and the developers have plugged any capability gaps that were holding you back before.

Self-service tech is helping save time in customer-facing businesses. More retailers are extending their use of self-checkout tills – with customers either scanning their items at the till and replacing the colleague, or going a step further and using technology to scan and bag as they go. Food outlets use interactive screens so customers place and pay for their own orders without a colleague having to stand with their fingers hovering over a button while the customer decides what flavour milkshake they want this time. Pre-ordering food and drink via an app in restaurants is also freeing up colleague time as the customer does the work of logging their own selection and processing the payment.

Done correctly, self-serve tech frees up significant colleague time while offering customers an enhanced experience. If you've checked in for a flight and got your boarding pass for your flight on your phone, you'll know what a better experience it is than joining a long queue at an airline desk to get your printed boarding pass. Where could freeing up your teams potentially save you money and make things better for the customer? The chances are the systems you will need to use are cheaper and better than last time you looked. If the numbers weren't quite good enough before, take another look and see if it has become a viable option.

Technology helps to keep your operation safe and legal too. For retailers, displaying the correct price to customers is a core requirement. Electronic shelf edge labels that show the price and any other useful customer information at the shelf have been widely used across Europe for years. Some countries have eye watering fines for items wrongly priced in shops. The risk of a huge fine in Scandinavia meant that the cost risk balance tipped in favour of buying expensive electronic shelf edge labels that also saved loads of colleague time. With electronic labels, a price change is implemented from head office at the touch of a button – no more printing tickets, ripping them off large sheets and walking round the shelves to put them out. No more price checking to double check the correct price ticket was out, it all happens automatically. As with a lot of technology hardware, the cost of the small screens that show the product price have fallen significantly. Rising hourly pay rates, challenges recruiting enough people in a tight labour market are making the time saving and cost trade-off more accessible even in markets without the huge fines.

Technology can do more than help save time.

Robot technology is being introduced to save colleague time too but it's not about the Star Wars type robots you might imagine! A robot is a machine that is programmed and designed to be good at one task. Examples include robot vacuum cleaners deployed in hotel rooms that are much better at getting into the corners and right under the bed every single time than their human counterparts. Robot vacuum cleaners are deployed in vast airport halls to keep them clean and tidy without needing an army of people with brushes. Even robot coffee machines have been developed so they grind the beans, make the coffee shot and then add the frothy milk and syrups. The new tech is called bean-to-cup and is driving a lot of the growth in coffee for sandwich shops and convenience outlets. It's a cost-effective way to provide a consistent, high-quality coffee without having to go through the training and on the job experience that it takes for a barista to be able to make the perfect coffee every time.

In warehouses, robots are used to work alongside a human partner, literally carrying the load and ensuring the most efficient route around the building is taken. These robots are used to increase the productivity of a human and do the heavy lifting that leads to fatigue and risks injury when done repeatedly over many shifts.

Anywhere that you have colleagues doing repetitive work, there is an opportunity for automation to play a part and chances are the cost-benefit equation will have changed since you last looked.

2. Behind the scenes tasks

The secret to effective time-saving is to understand what customers value. Knowing what matters to your customers so they come back again and again means you can protect and add to the things that customers come to you for – and then consider everything else as productivity improvement targets. Customers don't value your back-office tasks so all the things you do behind the scenes are great targets for timesaving.

It's worth looking out for times when your teams move more than is essential. This can be from reducing distances travelled in huge warehouses, to optimising workstations so everything a colleague needs for their work is close to hand.

3. Quick wins - are there ways you can accelerate the delivery of benefits in your existing plan?

If you can pull forward implementations, or phase them so you can unlock the bigger benefits earlier in the programme, it can be great way to find extra savings.

4. Outsourcing - are there things that an outside agency can do for you?

If you can find a service who make a speciality of more efficiently doing something you do, it can be a lower cost option for the same outcome. A benefit of outsourcing is that the service can often be rapidly implemented so if you are under pressure to find savings fast, outsourcing could be your friend.

One thing is certain. If you are being asked to find extra savings on top of your already prepared plan, you will need to find a different way of looking at things. Finding a fresh perspective can help you spot the opportunities you missed last time.

Case Studies – How others have found extra savings.

Proven innovative ways to deliver added value.

Example 1:

Concept stores. Retailers often miss a trick when designing a new format or concept store. Historically they would carefully consider the product offer and pore over every detail of the design and not give the same attention to the costs of operating the space. As staff costs have become a more important consideration, ways to save time are increasingly being designed into new customer concepts and stores. A regional co-op developed a small supermarket concept store to bring together all the labour-saving changes they could think of into a new store they were opening. It included optimising self-checkout solutions, a range of solutions to reduce time spent handling stock and the innovative use of audits and automation to help them with all the compliance tasks required of retail food businesses. Testing all the solutions together allowed them to see how they interacted. It showed the art of the possible and saved even more time than expected. The combined effect saved an extra 10% versus the savings they expected. It created a template for new stores and refits and showed them what would be viable changes to roll out across the whole estate.

New sites and refits offer a chance for new initiatives to be tried and understand the cumulative effect of testing everything together.

You don't want to end up with a patchwork estate. So although you might be trying some radical options, make sure they could be rolled out to all your sites. If it's something you think won't work in most of your sites perhaps it's not a good option to test? And consider how you could back out of it and make the store 'normal' again if needs be.

A word of caution – push yourself to be brave, but draw the line at reckless!

Example 2:

Measuring food prep time for a gourmet burger business showed they spent considerable time on the behind-the-scenes task of chopping veg, including potatoes for fries, and tomatoes and onions for burgers. The same fresh produce can be bought in ready-chopped, and the customer gets the same quality burger. Suppliers machine chopping produce in bulk quantities are more cost effective than hand chopping in each kitchen, ticking the box of saving back-of-house time while protecting quality and customer experience.

Example 3:

A retailer undertook work study that covered both the stores and the warehouses that supplied them. This study opened up opportunities to quantify trade-offs beyond the remit of any operational silos within the business. It looked at the impact of returned stock going back into the supply chain and how the way warehouses picked and stacked stock created extra work for store teams. The data created an evidence base for conversations that unlocked bigger benefits than either group could achieve alone.

When you are looking for new solutions, your brain is very good at discounting anything that seems too unusual or where you might have tried something similar before. There are many techniques you can use to get yourself into a different headspace that allows fresh thinking and to explore options in a new way. Run a session and allow yourselves to think the unthinkable. Expanding the horizons doesn't mean you should implement the craziest thing you can come up with. It's a way of breaking through some constraints and rigid corporate thinking to come up with some fresh ideas to unlock new ways of doing things.

Quick Wins – What you can do now.

If you are looking for extra productivity improvements beyond those already baked into your plans, you will probably need to be a bit more adventurous in looking at options than you may have already ruled out. It's time to feel brave…

● Use new site openings and refits as a testbed and opportunity to try something new. It can be insightful to see how multiple solutions come together and change your operating model.

● If new stores aren't an available testbed for you, look for other ways of doing small scale trials that allow you to learn quickly and move to rapid roll out.

● Can you create extra savings by delivering already planned benefits in a shorter timeline?

● Do a quick revisit of any tech solutions that were on the right track but didn't make the payback hurdle. Things might have changed that make the investment case stack up now.

● Don't forget to look at the costs outside of the salary budget. All the supplies your business uses could be sources of cost saving. Can you shorten till rolls and print them only when customers want them to save paper? What reports are printed out when they could be looked at on a mobile device? Are there heat, light and power saving options that could make a big impact given global energy price highs? Do teams really know how to operate for peak efficiency? Clue: if it has just gone out via a written message in email or on the intranet, there is probably more you can do.

Try some blue sky thinking and think the unthinkable.

Chapter 9:

Is the projected saving real?

Businesses are complex multi-team organisations, and what one part of the business does has an effect on other parts. The introduction of online services is a great example of a change that cuts across the whole organisation. Offering customers options to buy online requires cooperation from IT functions, supply teams, marketing, logistics, finance and operations. Online is so cross-functional that many organisations didn't know where it should sit in their structure to start with.

Most organisations have now found the right place for their online business, along with a seat at the most senior tables for their online leader. Often, despite many years of talking about it and trying, most businesses are not as slickly cross-functional as they could be, and this can impact how productivity improvement is addressed.

Understanding how changes in one part of the business affects others matters when you are trying to understand the costs and benefits of change programmes and initiatives. Those of us who have worked in Operations will know that it is the people at the point where your business meets the customer that too often have to pick up the consequences of change programmes that haven't worked out the full impact of the changes they are making.

It is Operations who deal with the unintended consequences of marketing programmes that drive a bigger customer response than expected, or have to deal with new loyalty schemes, and vouchers that have to be printed off. Taking HR systems online and replacing paper forms with digital data entry screens often adds extra operations time too. Time will be saved in a central data processing office while the extra work pushed to every supervisor leading a team can remain unseen. It is also Operations who have to deal with initiatives that aren't quite working yet or have plain gone wrong. To fully operationalise a change requires end-to-end thinking and an appreciation of the full impact of the change for every business department it touches.

Operational feedback can often be dismissed as negativity and baseless grumbles.

Running a multi-national business across different countries makes delivering a planned process change and savings delivery even more complex. There are differences between markets that range from small and subtle to huge variances that can cause big swings in the value created by a given change in different countries. There are often different rules and regulations that get in the way of global change roll out, even before you have considered cultural and customer variations. For example, a work force management programme designed to apply a universal approach to how rotas are planned and communicated quickly runs up against a tough mix of different laws governing how hours can be planned and any resulting change can be implemented.

From a corporate perspective, once the cost saving is baked into budgets, the saving has been made. The money has been banked, built into financial forecasts and is gone forever. But has that level of saving really been made, or is there some compensating and unfunded extra work happening somewhere?

Or even could the saving actually be bigger than first thought?

There is only one way to truly know what the time saving is and if the benefit case has been delivered. That is to measure the process pre and post the change.

How do I know what my project has really delivered?

The gold standard of understanding the change is to measure the process pre and post the change. It sounds like it will slow you down, add cost and just be plain dull, doesn't it? It doesn't have to be and some short, sharp focussed study during the testing stage will save time and money in the long run. There are lots of examples that demonstrate taking a hard look at process change in the beginning will deliver a better result in the end.

Any change always brings carries some emotional baggage with it. You will have a group of stakeholders each bringing their own perspective and set of prejudices to your project party. Onsite study brings data and logical thinking into the room, allowing you to sweep away some of the unhelpful emotion. You will have a clear evidence base to take into the next stage of roll out.

Improving a process does not always mean you can save time. That might sound illogical until you realise there can be a difference in the time saved on a process and whether you can realise any saving. For example, if we have a colleague working alongside a machine and we speed up the colleague's part of the process, unless the machine can increase its speed too, all we've done is create a short period of time when the colleague waits for the machine to catch up with the human.

Sometimes going a little slower to start allows you to be faster in your overall delivery.

It would be the same if you swapped out a colleague on a till for a self-checkout till that needed a colleague to be there in case the customer needed any help. You still need a person there – they are just slightly less busy than before. If you can swap out four tills and then need just one person to be on hand, then you have made a saving of three peoples' time.

If you have a site where you have to have two people onsite as a minimum to ensure safe working, no matter how many processes you take away you still have to pay for two people to be there.

A workload model that includes all the workload and minimum cover calculations for your business can really help to validate savings and highlight differences between theoretical savings you can calculate and the actual difference that can be realised.

The principles of delivering a saving are relatively simple. When you get into the nitty gritty and understand all the human and commercial factors that can affect delivery, it becomes no surprise that delivering genuine change and realising savings is trickier than it looks.

Case Studies – How others were able to review their improvements.

Validating benefit delivery is a great way of ensuring implementation meets its targets, or helping you find out where even more value exists.

Example 1:

New kit had been deployed in a warehouse to speed up order picking and optimise travel distance around the floor. Like most kit, it relied on a Wi-Fi signal to operate. A combination of high racking densely packed with stock and a large site meant that signal blackspots happened in the middle of aisles. This meant the tech lost its connection and instead of speeding up the process, colleagues were traveling extra distances in search of a Wi-Fi signal. The operations team had reported the signal drop issues, but until an independent study quantified the overall impact of poor Wi-Fi connection, the true size of the issue was not understood. As a result, Wi-Fi booster beacons were introduced so the planned benefit of the investment in expensive kit could be realised.

Example 2:

A retailer introduced a new format and associated staffing model for a service point in the store. The feedback from the trial stores was terrible and their complaints were centred around all the extra time that was pulled from the rest of the store because the new service model was not working. After a couple of days spent in each of a handful of stores, the measurement showed that the model worked beautifully when the new expert roles were present. The new model meant more time was spent with customers and other parts of the business were protected because the model worked so well. However, when the expert was unexpectedly off sick, they were not replaced and the resource gap created such a pull on other parts of the business that customer service overall suffered and colleagues were struggling to deliver their usual service levels. The finding meant that instead of walking away from what was generally a good solution all together, the project team knew they had to find a solution for covering absence.

Example 3:

A coffee shop chain were looking at design options for a new counter to go into their outlets. Design projects are often hampered by opinions and personal preferences rather than being shaped by robust, evidence-based decision making. The process so far had whittled the designs down to three possible counter layouts. The business built a mock-up of each counter and ran through a day's orders

A multi million pound spend on a design-based project.

from a real store to see how they would fare. They also called in experts to measure how long tasks took behind each of the counters. As a result, they proved which design was the optimum and which ones looked good on paper but slowed down colleagues working hard to serve customers. The evidence base allowed them to create a best-in-class counter design and to invest millions on new counters safe in the knowledge that they had a design that looked good for the brand and that created an efficient workspace too.

Quick Wins – What you can do now.

A few days of time and motion measurement can bring quick wins for any project, creating insights and observations that are difficult to learn any other way. The quick wins below can be used successfully alongside time and motion measurement or when measurement is a no go.

- If the project has cross-functional impact, involve each function all the way through. It will help you develop the best solution from the start and avoid unwelcome surprises from a disgruntled stakeholder later in the project.

- Someone in the business may have measured the process you are looking at before. Track down any data and know-how available to help you more accurately estimate the opportunity you are addressing.

- Learning from others who have done similar projects about the benefit they realised. It might be a peer in a similar business you don't directly compete with, or a business operating in a different sector facing into a parallel challenge.

- Vendors can also be a useful source of advice and support. If you are buying kit, the vendor will have lots of experience of helping build a business case and existing customers you can talk to.

Chapter 10:

How can I budget better?

Different teams within an organisation will have their own definition of what makes a good salary budget. Finance teams want the numbers to stack up to a top line number agreed by the executive. Individual outlets want the number to be as big as possible! If you are responsible for budget allocation, you want to make the best decisions you can from the available funds. You'll want the money to be fairly spread so any budgetary challenge is felt equally. The money should be allocated in line with company priorities and to where there the best opportunities are.

There are broadly two approaches to budgeting. One is a 'last year plus' method, where budgets are based on what sites spent last year – plus or minus an agreed percentage for the coming year. This is a quick and simple approach but does not always produce an equitable result. Historical budget imbalances are perpetuated and broad-brush application of a percentage does not accurately reflect site specific operational challenges that may create extra work. For example, if stock has to be moved multiple floors in a lift, it will take longer to handle the delivery than in a one floor site. Or if linked to sales, a unit selling many low-priced items will have more stock handling work to do than a similar unit that sells fewer higher priced items, even if the top line sales number is the same.

The more accurate way to budget is to allocate salary hours and spend on what are called bottom-up workload calculations.

Bottom up workload models calculate the work associated with each task on a site-by-site basis and add up the total time from all the separate tasks. It sounds complicated, but workload calculation models can do the heavy lifting for you. Basing workload on task level calculations linked to sales targets for the coming year overcomes many of the fairness issues that dog the cost-plus budget allocation method. Each site is rebased for workload and the associated budget they need to deliver their sales targets. Workload models can be built to reflect any operational variance that exists across the organisation and budgets can be periodically adjusted to reflect unit performance versus their sales target.

In many businesses, the total calculated from bottom-up workload numbers rarely matches the allowed budget number signed off by the executive team. The number from the exec is known as the top-down number. When the gap between top-down and bottom-up is relatively small, it is easy make small adjustments to bring the numbers together. When the gap is large it becomes a harder decision for senior teams to decide where to focus their salary investment and how the challenge should be spread. At least the model means unpleasant trade-off decisions are made in a transparent way.

Budgeting sits somewhere between an art and a science. It starts as a negotiation between finance and the other business functions of how much sales, salary and other costs and margins are balanced across functions within the organisation. If operational leads are going into discussions with a budget bid based on a robust workload calculation, it adds weight to the negotiations. It is an approach that is likely to be more compelling for hardheaded finance leads, than an emotion-led request.

Another significant benefit of a model is that it allows you to know how cost is spread across different tasks and accurately cost the impact of changes. For example, what would be the true cost of increasing turnover by 5%? How much cash would it release if you stopped stock counts? What would be the salary cost differential if you took out tills and replaced them with self-checkout units and one person to provide till cover? All these scenarios can be modelled and the cost impact calculated more accurately than using simple assumptions for your top line business case.

If workload models sound a good bet, what is involved?

Workload models

Models add up the time required for all the separate tasks your teams do in a way that reflects your operation and the variance across your estate. For example, by knowing how long it takes to put an item on the shelf and the number of items handled by a site, the model can calculate the workload on an annual, monthly and weekly basis. If some sites have to use a lift, have an offsite stock room, or are required to fill out extra customs form, this can all be reflected in the model.

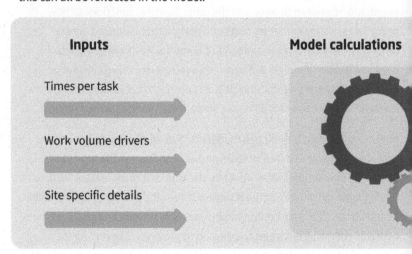

Inputs

Times per task

Work volume drivers

Site specific details

Model calculations

The model will run a series of calculations for each task and add them up to give a total. Activities such as training and some management tasks are best modelled by creating a rule that will drive the time required for them – you might want to fund one hour's training each month for every person. You might want site managers to be free to manage all the time, while supervisors might spend half their time on core tasks. These simple rules can be built into the model so all the activities completed by the onsite team are reflected in the workload calculations.

If you are moving to workload-based models for the first time, it will take at least as much work engaging people in the new way of working as it does to build the model. You'll need to create a core steering group to review the

> **As with any project, building the model is only part of the work.**

Outputs

Workload hours and costs by unit, by week

Equitable allocation of available budget

Impact assessment of "what if" changes

model as it develops and a communication plan to build confidence and buy in to the numbers. Experience shows that the steering group works best when it is made up of the people known to be 'budget nerds' from across the business. If the people who always dig through every last bit of budget detail feel it is fair, it will build confidence with everyone else. Remember, you are not wanting everyone to be happy, as cost budgets are usually lower than numbers that would make people smile! You are aiming for a fair and accurate way to allocate the available funds across your estate.

You will also need a governance group to sign off and oversee changes. This is not as onerous as it sounds. It is having a senior group who ensures changes are fair and realistic. The model will be made up of hard facts – like number of customers served, and assumptions – like the training and management ones above. Increasing training to an hour a week instead of a month might be an admirable intention, but does the person proposing it have the sign-off rights for spending the extra money?

You need to have enough structure, so the model remains fair and transparent without becoming bogged down in bureaucracy.

Case Studies: How others have budgeted effectively.

Combining data and logic helps businesses make better decisions about how they invest salary budgets.

Example 1:

A chain of grocery stores moved from a cost-plus model where budgets were based on previous year spent to a workload-based model. While the majority of stores' budgets remained close to what they would have received through the old process, there was more subtle variance in allocation. For example, of two stores with similar top line sales and close early budgets, started to diverge as the store with significantly more workload, related to the instore bakery and sandwich making, was allocated more salary budget than the store selling more packaged goods from the shelves.

Some stores had benefited from historical over-allocation and had been afforded a degree of salary budget protection that the workload did not justify, so started to transition to lower budget numbers.

The model was used to create a glide path to ideal spend while balancing the books.

Example 2:

A retail chain extensively used their new model to create different cost scenarios and estimate the cost impact of operational changes they were considering. The model helped them prioritise changes based on the benefit they would deliver and undertake extensive desktop testing before taking any expensive action. Their model was a great way of considering the impact of more radical changes and encouraged the generation of more innovative changes that would be more difficult to try out in real life.

Example 3:

A warehouse team used estimation and experience to gauge how many hours effort were needed to pick, pack and despatch each order they were presented with. This worked well for some of the time but meant sometimes too many or too few hours were allocated, and if the experienced person who knew how to estimate was away, the operation did not run well.

Rather than create a full annual budget model, the business used the times for each task measured during work study to create a simple Excel file, meaning they could more accurately calculate the hours needed for each order. It also helped understand bottle necks in the operation, based on the number of people available for the most complex part of the process.

With the model, they are able to make better workload planning choices, so throughput and resources are better matched.

Previously, workflows could be lumpy, with periods of high pressure alternating with downtime, causing order delays through the bottleneck.

Quick Wins – What can I do now?

● Make sure modelled hours match the available budget – they need to be aligned.

● Keep the model simple and avoid unnecessary complexity. Over complexity makes it harder to maintain, update and explain.

● Avoid a black box model where you don't have visibility of the logic used to deliver the output. Make calculations and logic transparent to make buy-in easier.

Keep your model up to date. It needs to reflect changes in your business and process.

Artificial intelligence

Letting the genie out of the bottle.

In the time since we started writing this book to near publication date, in late summer 2023, AI has moved from a relatively niche topic to something most of us are aware of and many will have used.

Two big news stories have broken, the release of ChatGPT and a letter signed by more than 1,000 people warning of potential risks to society and civilisation by human-competitive AI systems in the form of economic and political disruptions.

AI has been used in many applications to date and what has made ChatGPT grab so many headlines is that it is a language-based model. ChatGPT is a very sophisticated chat bot. You have probably interacted with simple chat bots providing on-demand customer service on many websites and apps, where the 'conversation' is tightly scripted and based on logical routing to help you achieve what you need to do. When your query diverts from the script, you are passed to a human agent to resolve things.

ChatGPT is different from these routed interactions. ChatGPT doesn't just spit out a line of text to a defined prompt, it can write an essay or poetry, translate and summarise text and even generate business ideas.

> # Like all versatile tools, humankind can use it for good or evil.

The ability to generate content from information scraped from the internet that may or may not be genuine creates genuine concern about the capability to create deep fakes that can mislead whole populations.

It is the ability to potentially do harm with AI that prompted the non-profit Future of Life Institute to issue a letter calling for a six month pause and ask that "AI labs and independent experts should use this pause to jointly develop and implement a set of shared safety protocols for advanced AI design and development that are rigorously audited and overseen by independent outside experts".

There are huge societal, moral, and legal issues still to be resolved with AI development that are important and will impact all of us. We'd like to set those aside while we consider how AI is likely to affect operational productivity as it becomes more integrated into industry.

1. Contact centres

Contact centres have been evolving for many years from all telephone-based operations to integrating live chat and social media channels. Simple chat bots are widely used in service centres so some customer journeys are completed without any human intervention. Or chat bots are used to do the initial data gathering so that when a human is needed the time taken is shorter. This core productivity principle of focusing people where they make a difference is likely to be stretched further as language-based solutions will be able to take on more tasks that currently need a human to complete them. How quickly this will happen is hard to tell. It used to be a long process to get a chatbot set up that provided a good customer experience. As with all technology applications, the time to configure and set up a service has reduced. Early adopters using new technology will do the hard learning that followers will benefit from.

It is easy to see how issue resolution will be a fertile ground for AI. It will be more interesting to see how it plays out into sales situations. Many contact centres offer a mix of customer services alongside teams looking to sign you up for a new contract or add services to an existing one. For example, many of us now have home broadband from our mobile phone provider as a result of sales conversations. It is easy to see that AI will be able to effectively identify potential sales targets and perhaps we will move away from the blanket selling approaches that can annoy many consumers. Will it need the human touch to close the deal? And if so, which deals? It remains to be seen.

AI technology means contact centres will either have more capacity to reduce queues and take on new service offerings or will need fewer people. It will also make it easier for contact centre specialist services to offer support for a range of brands in a single super service centre. It will require careful consideration of how a brand delivers a unique brand experience as more tech is introduced and if contact centres amalgamate.

Productivity is delivering your brand effectively, so every change you make must fit with delivery of your brand proposition.

2. Warehousing

Warehousing has been an early adopter of robotics in general and, as discussed earlier, the trend to reduce human movement time and automate stock movement as much as possible is set to continue. Warehousing is likely to be affected by the general business trend to use digitisation and automation to reduce back-office work and streamline admin workflows.

3. Offices

The drive to integrate data from different sources to create simpler workflows with less manual intervention will continue and hopefully accelerate. From our work in office settings, a challenge faced by many is suboptimal user interfaces and screens. To date, data entry has been centred on a human inputting data in a way that works for data-led systems. The development of more language-based systems will hopefully lead to better interfaces that provide the systems with the data they need while being much easier to use for humans where their input is needed.

4. Retail Self-service

This is a growing trend in customer-facing businesses where self-checkout technology is already changing retail stores. AI should enable a better customer experience and continue the drive to more self-service. A challenge for retail is how the front end of the store needs to change to efficiently deliver what customers need with a mix of tech and people. As the days of long till banks and big cash-taking colleague teams are going, what does that mean for leadership structures? If the number of customers needing human help reduces, how do retailers avoid having colleagues spending significant time waiting for customers? Again, brands will need to consider what their brand service proposition is and how technology and people work together to deliver it.

For retailers handling large volumes of stock, the hope is that AI helps improve the ability to accurately predict sales to an increasingly granular level. A significant driver of extra work in retail is stock that won't fit to the shelf directly from the delivery but must go back to a storage area and be reworked at a future time. More accurate stock requirement predictions should enable a higher proportion of 'just in time' stock deliveries to reduce stock holding in stores. Instore stock management processes are likely to be simplified too. For a glimpse of what the future could look like, visit an Amazon Go store where technology monitors shelf fill. There is no need to do gap checks or write out fill up lists, the system just tells you what you need to fetch from back stock as soon as it is needed.

Better forecasting of customer numbers should also help with tighter rotas that flex resource to match peaks in demand more accurately. However, to achieve this will need a more flexible approach to hours worked than many retailers currently achieve with their permanent store teams. Flexible hours tend to be associated with short notice changes to working patterns that can be difficult to manage for many. If better forecasting led to more notice of flexible working hours that might make a variable work pattern a manageable option for more people.

5. Quick serve restaurants

Food outlets and coffee shops should benefit from many of the changes that affect retail, such as more automation in back-office systems and better forecasting to plan colleague resource. Quick serve food outlets are all about maximising capacity at peak while avoiding excessive downtime outside of peak times and this core productivity challenge is likely to be unchanged. Smarter and more targeted marketing campaigns might help manage the demand and help broaden the peaks rather than create bigger spikes in demand.

Self-service options for placing orders are being adopted in many food outlets and if smarter AI can offer a better customer experience, many of the brands that have been reluctant to try self-ordering are more likely to give it a go.

It is easy to predict that back-office tasks will be reduced and better forecasting will lead to more accurate planning for stock and people. It is also clear that demand for that one-to-one personal service will still exist. We might do most of our shopping via an app and home delivery, yet still want to browse the food stalls at a farmers market and discuss which cheese, wine, or other artisan produced delicacy we'd like to try. Top end restaurants will still exist and there will be situations where only a human will do.

The unknowable bit is how far and how fast the middle ground will move. Will we all be out of a job and have endless hours of leisure time as has been wrongly predicted for tech for years? Or will having a human-led service model be a way to cut through a host of reliably good and ultimately unengaging AI led brand interactions? We suspect anything we write now will look horribly outdated in a remarkable short period of time. However things go, the principle of finding ways to deliver your unique brand promise more efficiently is the route to success. As productivity professionals we are going to have a whole host of extra tools to work with that should create new opportunities for us. Perhaps brand strategists will have a tougher time. Trying to differentiate your brand in a world where tech tends to homogenise experiences will be a considerable challenge.

Final thoughts

We've covered a lot of productivity ground together. At its simplest, productivity is about doing more with the same or less. If you are starting afresh in an organisation that has not considered efficiency and productivity before, you will find loads of opportunities, and the challenge will be deciding the order to implement them to deliver best value. The more normal situation is to be looking for the next set of savings in a business that has worked hard at their productivity agenda for several years.

Productivity opportunities vary by sector too. In hospitality it is about maximising your capacity at peak while minimising downtime at quiet times. In warehousing, pick rates and travel distances are key. For retailers it's a mix of having efficient stock processes and carefully matching resource to demand, especially at the busiest and quietest times.

Whatever sector and challenge you are facing there are nine key facts to remember:

1. Productivity is about delivering the brand effectively, so every change you make must fit with delivery of your brand proposition.

2. Driving productivity in the organisation needs to be someone's job and they might need budget to bring in external experts too.

3. Without senior manager support, the resources needed to deliver and sustain change will not be there.

4. There is no monopoly on good ideas – look at your sector, other sectors, and ask colleagues working in the processes, they can all be sources of time savings.

5. There is a community of productivity professionals out there, both virtually and in real life – join them and you will have an endless source of ideas and learnings that make you more productive.

6. Look across the whole operation to unlock productivity – cross-functional savings can be bigger than you expect.

7. Implementing change can be harder and may take longer than you might first think – especially if it involves technology and system changes.

8. Creating and maintaining a high productivity organisation is a continuous journey – a productivity expert's work is never done.

9. Stay close to your operations so you make changes that work in the real world and not just in a theoretical ivory tower.

Good luck with your productivity journey, wherever your roadmap takes you.

About Rethink Productivity:

Founded in 2011, ReThink delivers great data that surfaces insights to create better decisions and discover opportunities for positive change.

Our client base covers all sectors where people and processes matter, such as retail, hospitality, warehousing, and the contact centre business, and ensuring a good match of people to workload is an essential part of our ongoing success. We at ReThink have also used our tried and trusted techniques for a wider range of clients - from funeral directors to offices processing payroll, from account managers leading a sales push to many aspects of airport operations. Having provided productivity insights to some of the largest blue-chip companies, as well as to small startups, we have completed work across the globe.

The ReThink team specialise in using a range of workstudy techniques to create a fresh view on productivity opportunities that allow businesses to take action and make a difference.

We are so passionate about the power of data and the importance of capturing and using it in the best way that in 2019 we launched ReTime, our own app-based software for accurate onsite data capture. ReTime is used on every ReThink project and by a growing number of independent work study professionals and companies. In 2023 we went a step further and set up ReTime Academy. Through the academy we provide training to people wanting to become qualified work study analysts and offer an annual refresher course that all qualified time and motion experts complete to ensure consistency of data over time. We are proud to be training the next generation of productivity professionals.

Our data passion extends to developing benchmark data sets that bring an extra perspective for our clients. With over 7 million data points, we bring useful context to the measurements we take for any business.

Recognising the power of data, we have broken new ground in becoming the first remote working UK business to be selected to set up a three-way Knowledge Transfer Partnership with Portsmouth University and Innovate UK. We are working together to create an advanced benchmarking solution using AI and machine learning.

Time and motion studies sound to some like an old fashioned and outdated approach. We think it is a fantastic source of robust data that used the right way will unlock productivity and contribute to innovation and ongoing success.

If you'd like to find out more, check out **www.rethinkproductivity.co.uk**.

Notes

Notes

Notes

Notes